T0162301

Modern-Day Selling

The Keys to Unlocking Your Hidden
Potential and Reconnecting You with
Your Customers

Modern-Day Selling

The Keys to Unlocking Your Hidden
Potential and Reconnecting You with
Your Customers

Brian Barfield

**BUSINESS
BOOKS**

Winchester, UK
Washington, USA

First published by Business Books, 2012
Business Books is an imprint of John Hunt Publishing Ltd., Laurel House, Station Approach,
Alresford, Hants, SO24 9JH, UK
office1@jhpbooks.net
www.johnhuntpublishing.com

For distributor details and how to order please visit the 'Ordering' section on our website.

Text copyright: Brian Barfield 2011

ISBN: 978 1 78099 457 4

A CIP catalogue record for this book is available from the British Library.

Design: Stuart Davies

Printed in the USA by Edwards Brothers Malloy

We operate a distinctive and ethical publishing philosophy in all
areas of our business, from our global network of authors to
production and worldwide distribution.

CONTENTS

Introduction and Overview

The world as we know it has changed drastically over the years. Unfortunately, the styles and concepts of professional selling have not been able to keep up with such a changing environment. We currently find ourselves struggling to find a greater success because our customers have evolved. The stresses and demands of the world today have created a void within our customers that has yet to be explored. This has made the sales floor a much tougher environment for today's sales associates. Long gone are the days of easy sales waiting to be had. In today's selling world there is a need for change. What we need today is an awakening of the ways we sell and how we treat the modern-day customer. In order to do this the modern-day sales professional must be born.

Owners and managers across the country have found themselves struggling to find these few elite sales professionals. They are looking for that diamond in the rough that will transform their stores and impact their environment in a powerful way. Unfortunately, many stores never seem to find these elite sales professionals and are left in a constant state of mediocrity. Sales associates come, and they go, but nothing really changes. Why is this?

There are many reasons why today's stores do not reach their full potential. The economy is certainly a contributing factor, but is very over-used as an excuse for mediocrity. Today's sales professionals are not being given any new insight and vision to build upon the successes of the past. The days of greeting, asking open-ended questions, overcoming objections and closing will no longer lead you to lasting success. What we need is a revolutionary insight that will bring change to the modern-day sales floor. Now is the time to take what is good and make it great. This is the secret to finding a lasting success.

This book is designed to be a road map for the modern-day sales professional to achieve a higher level of success. The first step towards success is to understand who you truly are as a sales professional. You must find the true purpose and meaning of your calling in the sales world. By learning the power of self-examination you will be given the keys to unlock the hidden potential within. If you understand what the modern-day sales professional should look like you will then have the vision and insight to give yourself the proper makeover necessary to make an impact in people's lives. This will allow you to brand yourself in a way that sets you apart from every other sales professional in your area.

The next important insight is to learn who the modern-day customer is and how to properly meet their needs. Over the years we have been trained on the four basic personality types. This training is very effective in helping you to understand people. The problem is that the pressures and demands of the world today mean that our customers are in a constant state of change. Without simplifying things you will not be able to meet their needs by following the demands of a set personality pattern. Today's sales associates need to be prepared to serve every customer as they are when they arrive in the store. You will find that today's customers will vary in four basic ways: Demanding, Analytical, Guarded and Simple Minded. Learning who they are and how to sell them properly is vital to your success.

Once you understand who the modern-day customer is, you will discover the void I spoke about earlier. Today's customers want more than just a professional sales presentation. They want to be entertained and given an experience that leaves them coming back for more. It is here that you will learn the importance of serving your customers while selling. There are many different ways that you can serve your customers. We will focus on creating a show for them and giving them an entertaining experience. This insight on performing while selling will give you a new-found meaning of success. This chapter will also teach you to value your customers and put their needs first above all else. These skills will help to create a special bond of trust between you and your customer. This will help you create a foundation of a loyal customer base.

Moving along we will turn our attention to the skill of managing your sales presentation. In order to be successful on today's sales floor you will need to become more efficient, and effective, with your sales presentation. There is so much to do, and so little time to do it. Therefore it is important to understand the concept of managing your sale. This will help you find a balance in creating an amazing customer experience and will free up your time to be more productive. You will learn the importance of rhythm and timing so that you are not selling too little or too much. We will also look at ways to cut out the fat of your sales presentation so that your sales become more lean and productive.

Once you have learned to manage your sales presentation, we will look at ways for you to become an effective closer. It is a very sad fact that many sales associates do not understand how to close a sale. This chapter will teach you how to jump into the close with your customer. With you as their instructor and guide through the sales process, your customer will establish a trust that will make closing the easiest part of the sales presentation. When you put your customer's needs first, and build a bond of trust, closing will never be the same again. This chapter will help you become lethal and effective in your closing style and technique.

The next step we will discuss is very important to finding long-lasting success. It is important to build a strong customer base that is loyal and dedicated to you. Closing a sale is great, but the secret to lasting success is having a strong customer base. In this chapter you will learn ways to create a sense of obligation for your customers to shop with you. How nice would it be to have customers waiting for you and not wanting anyone else to help them? Could you imagine a sale that only took a few minutes every time? It is possible. I see it every day with the customer base I have built over the last seven years of my selling career. It is here that sales become easy, when you create a steady flow of income that seems almost effortless.

These new concepts and selling styles are proven techniques to give your customer a unique and fulfilling experience. On my journey to becoming a yearly million dollar sales associate, it was these treasures that I discovered that brought me my success. It is important to understand that we all take different journeys through our careers. Being able to look back and see your journey with clarity is an important part of moving forward to lasting success. It is here that you will be given fresh insight to explore your journey and understand the true meaning and purpose of your sales career.

Once you see your journey with clarity it will allow you the opportunity to discover and unlock your hidden potential. I believe that every sales associate has hidden potential that has yet to be discovered. Learning to follow the light of truth will lead you to the founding principles of modern-day selling. Our forefathers built the foundation of our selling empire with pure values of trust, honesty and integrity. Over the years greed has led us astray with empty promises of prosperity. It has severed the bond of trust between sales associate and customer. This is why we find such resistance on the sales floor today. Thus we entered the era of bad sales tactics used to manipulate and deceive our customers in purchasing.

Now, a new day is dawning, and there is a message of hope spreading light to the sales floor. For too long people have led empty careers with no vision and insight to true satisfaction. Change is coming to the sales floor as we now unlock the full potential of true success. Getting back to the things that once made our industry great is essential to finding purpose and meaning in your life once again. Now is the time to reunite sales associate and customer, and bring back integrity to the sales floor. The new era of Modern-Day Selling has begun.

The final key ingredient to becoming a modern-day sales professional is to implement what you have learned and maintain it. I think everyone has witnessed the following scenario. A sales associate attends a wonderful sales training. A fire is ignited within and they come back ready to rule the sales floor. Great things appear to be happening as their figures rise and all seems well. Fast forward a month or two and they are back in their old ways. All the success they discovered has suddenly vanished. A true sales professional will maintain and build upon the foundation of their success. They are always moving forward and finding new success.

In closing I believe this book will give you a new vision and insight to find success as a modern-day sales professional. These new concepts are the materials you will need to build upon the strong foundation that has already been laid. With the proper instruction and guidance you will be able to build your own creation of success. My goal is to teach these modern-day sales professionals, and give them these new tools to enable them to find greater success. After all, you are now my customers and it is time for me to give you the ultimate experience you deserve. So turn the page and let's get started on your journey to new success.

Chapter 1

Birth of the Modern-Day Sales Professional

In today's stores many sales associates are struggling to find their identity. The training they receive often gives them a vision of success without a proper road map to guide them through the process. This has led to a generation of sales associates who hunger for knowledge and guidance to go along with a vision and a plan. These sales associates are full of potential, with skills that lie buried within just waiting to be found. It is when these skills are discovered that the modern-day sales professional is born.

Anyone who has ever had a child will tell you that the day their child was born was one of the most memorable moments of their life. Being a father myself I can tell you that the first moment you hold your child is exhilarating and unforgettable. In an instant your life is changed forever. As you discover your skills I challenge you to treat them just like a newborn child. Nurture your new-found skills and watch over them so nothing can separate you from your future.

Sadly, many sales professionals do not know the proper ways to nurture and grow these new-found skills. Without the proper care and maintenance bad habits will begin to take root. Like a weed these bad habits will slowly begin to choke the life out of these new-found skills. Just as in childhood this is the time that a young sales professional is most vulnerable. They are not able to fully understand, or see things as clearly as an adult. This is where the guidance of a store manager or well-rooted sales professional can guide them through the beginning stages of becoming a modern-day sales professional. It is the maturity and experience that gives these mentors the insight and vision to see the road ahead and protect them from upcoming dangers. Without the proper guidance the chances of survival would be very slim for any young sales professional.

As you read the previous paragraph did anyone come to mind that had potential but was not yet strong enough to survive? Even better, could this be you? The good news is that it is never too late to be reborn. A fresh start is all you need. With a new-found dedication and a vision of where you want to go the sky is the limit. With the proper guidance and a willingness to implement what you learn, great things are ahead of you. A career filled with success and prosperity awaits you.

Now is the time to define who you are as a sales professional. It all starts with a renewed passion and a purpose. The more you understand who you should become the better your sales career will be. By learning and implementing your new-found skill, success will follow in due course. As people see your success they will want to learn and look up to you. Now you have become a leader who impacts the store in a dynamic way bringing energy and excitement. Promotions may come. Career paths may open. I promise you that your life will be changed in a profound way.

Whatever level of sales professional you may be there is one thing that is vital. I call it branding yourself as a sales professional. It will define who you are as a sales professional and what you are all about. It is important to recognize that everyone is not the same. We are all unique and different as we walk down the path towards success. Find out what works for you and make the necessary changes to reach your full potential. Set a brand of who you are with excellence and superior customer service.

When you think of Rolex, Hearts on Fire or Tacori, what comes to mind? Many people would think about quality and excellence. They are recognized as being some of the best brands in the industry. They have worked hard to brand themselves in a way that sets them apart from most of their competition. In order to be an elite sales professional your customers must see you in the same light as these great companies. Take the time to look into your favorite jewelry brand's history. Study and learn how they achieved success. I can assure you that they did not show up on the market with a product and ask a premium price. They all started with a vision and a plan for success. Then they strived for greatness by building on that foundation with superior quality. For many branded companies the times were tough in the early days. With persistence and a belief in what they were doing they climbed to higher heights. The key is they never gave up or looked back.

The question is, how do your brand yourself in a way that sets you apart from every other sales associate? What will make your customers loyal to you? In order to get a clear vision of who you should become you must first learn the importance of self-examination. Take the time to look into the mirror of your soul and see yourself as others do. What do you see when you open up your mind for self-examination? What areas will you admit that you need help in? Are you happy with your performance? Do you see a potential for greater success? Are you willing to do what it takes to become an elite sales professional? These are the questions you must ask yourself before you can move on any further in this process.

Have you ever witnessed a co-worker who goes to an amazing sales seminar and comes back ready to rule the sales floor? They hit the sales floor with passion and excitement. Great things appear to be happening. Their sales increase as well as their confidence. Fast forward a month or two and everything has changed. They are back to their bad habits and nothing has really changed. Without examining themselves often they forgot what they were supposed to look like and in the process became ugly again.

This may sound funny, but try going a week without looking in a mirror. Without being able to see yourself you would become a mess. Can you imagine how your hair would look (if you have hair)? Suddenly those blemishes you can't see or maintain begin to get worse. You would have no clue because you cannot see them. Your manager might point it out to you but could you really fix it without seeing what you are doing? No! Being able to see yourself honestly gives you a huge advantage to achieving success.

There is one thing to keep in mind as you learn the power of looking in the mirror. Make sure you are honest with yourself in what you see. There is nothing more embarrassing than someone unattractive looking in the mirror and seeing themselves as beautiful. The only thing worse is that American Idol contestant who auditions and thinks they can sing when really they sound horrible. It is a train wreck in the making unless you put the brakes on your ego and get control of yourself. Don't be the laughing stock and butt of every joke at the water cooler.

To those of you who are looking in the mirror and see potential for a makeover I commend you. It is the first step to real change that is lasting. It is time for an extreme seller makeover. Have you ever watched the TV show where they take an overweight person and transform them into someone beautiful? It is truly amazing. You are always so happy for that person because you have watched them work so hard throughout the show. All the long workouts, abstaining from bad foods, and time spent focused on getting fit. They paid a price and did what had to be done to get results. It was not handed to them. They were away from their families and went through peaks and valleys to reach the promised land. It can all be yours if you are willing to pay the price for success. Getting there won't be easy but I promise you that in the end you will love the results. So will all your co-workers and customers. They won't even recognize you and will be amazed at how you have transformed.

Chapter 2

Signs of Elite Sales Professionals

In order to become great we must first learn what greatness looks like. What makes someone an elite sales professional? For those of you who have been in the business for a while I am sure you have witnessed an amazing sales professional at some point during your career. I have worked with, and managed, many great people during my career. They have all had an impact on what I have achieved today. However, there is only one sales professional who blew me away and left me searching for answers that I eventually found. It was over the one and a half years that I worked alongside this elite sales professional that little treasures were given to me along the way. It changed my career forever.

I remember the first time I met Ty. I was managing a store that had two other sister stores in the same mall. Ty was interviewing down the hall and I was asked to come down and interview him and see what I thought. The person I met did not have the traditional image of a sales professional. He was well dressed but had a long blonde braided pony-tail that went completely down his back. After talking for a while he informed me that he had been the drummer of a hard rock band that was somewhat successful. I had actually heard of the band, but did I really want a rocker selling my customers? I was hesitant to hire Ty and decided to pass him on to a fellow manager. This was a big mistake.

Within a couple of weeks the store down the hall began to have really big sales days. It was Ty! He was closing sales at a rapid pace and winning over customers that had previously been in my store. How could this be? He had never sold jewelry before. In short he was kicking our butt. We were no match for him. As I told you before success will bring promotion, and it did for Ty. I was glad to see him go but still curious as to how he did it. The natural thing to think is that he was cheating by discounting or doing something illegal, not respecting company guidelines. I would get to find out first-hand in about a year.

Things in life always happen for a reason. At the time you may not know why or understand, but in time it usually becomes crystal clear. This is one of those moments. I was going through a personal crisis and decided to step down until something opened up closer to home. So I was transferred to the largest store in the market to work as an assistant manager. Really I was just there to sell but needed the title to justify my pay. It was by the grace of God Almighty that Ty was also working in this store. Now I would have a chance to figure things out.

I watched as he sold customer after customer. No matter who came in or how tough they appeared to be they were no match for Ty. It was as if he hypnotized these people with his words and calm demeanor. The bottom line was that everyone left loving Ty. They would wait for him with a loyalty that was unmatched. What was he doing that made him so successful? He was so efficient and could close quicker than anyone I had ever seen. Everything seemed effortless on his part. I had to know his secret.

Ty was a private person who loved his family. He never really opened up to others and shared the secrets to his success. It was years later that I discovered his secrets. He had found a way to understand all his customers. No matter who they were he always knew how to sell them. He was able to meet their needs and leave them feeling better than when they walked in the door. This skill mixed with product knowledge was lethal.

The other thing I learned from Ty was how to put on a show for your customer. It was a simple formula. Relax the customer, gain their trust, then meet their needs and become their friend. People left feeling like they were special and kept coming back for more. He genuinely cared for his customers. I owe a lot of my success to witnessing such perfection on the sales floor. Thank you, Ty.

Over the years I got burnt out managing and found my way out of the mall market. Through a twist of fate in one of the worst moments of my career a new door opened. Always remember that everything happens for a reason. I will share the story with you later in the book. I found myself working at the most reputable high-end jewelry store in town. It was a locally owned store and did not have all the restrictions and guidelines that bigger companies have. It is here I began to discover those precious treasures that Ty had buried within me many years ago.

The first thing I did was to find a way to use my nine years of management experience and start managing myself. The first sign of an elite sales professional is their ability to manage themselves. They do not need a store manager to lead them or guide them along the way. I want to be clear that respect for a store manager should always be present. After all, they are in charge for a reason. When you manage yourself things get done before the manager even asks you to do something. You use your vision and insight to always be one step ahead of the game. If a manager is smart he will leave you alone, especially if you are producing positive results.

The second sign of an elite sales professional is that they have a vision and plan of where they want to go. They will set their own goals before any goal is given. This goes beyond sales dollars. They are thinking about their customers and how to meet their needs. The elite sales professional will always be thinking ahead and planning for their future. If you have ever worked with an elite sales professional you will have noticed they always seem to be one step ahead of everyone else. This is because they are always planning for the future and looking at the path ahead. They are prepared to go in whatever direction opportunity takes them.

The next sign of an elite sales professional is that they under-stand their customers. Just like Ty, they seem to have the answers for any personality type. In the next chapter we will dig deeper into this area because it is so important. Did you know that mastering this will allow you to outsell those product gurus? Product knowledge is important but knowing how to treat people should be your top priority. My weakest area of product knowledge is Rolex watches. For some reason I have never taken the time to study as deeply as I should. We have two experts in our store that know a lot more about Rolex than I do. That is an area I am working on as we speak. Can you guess who is number one in Rolex sales at our store? It's me. It's not always about what you know but how you make people feel.

Another significant sign of an elite sales professional is that they are always learning and growing. Then they implement what they have learned and find a way to maintain it. The self-examination that I spoke of in the last chapter is one tool that is used to succeed in growing. They will also be willing to exper-iment and try out new ideas and concepts. It could be a selling style, new product knowledge, or advice they received from someone they respect. They will watch others sell and look for the things that make them successful. Then they will add it into their arsenal of sales weaponry and they become the Rambo's of the sales floor.

If you have ever witnessed an elite sales professional in action it is awesome. Their sales presentation is near flawless as they have their customer's complete attention and trust. Even if they make a mistake it is so smooth that it is hardly noticed or quickly forgiven. It seems unfair because they get away with things that would doom a normal sales associate in their sale. The main reason for this is perfecting their sales presentation and always adapting it to mirror their customer.

Finally the last sign of an elite sales professional is the way they make everyone else around them better. They are the leaders of the store who bring energy and excitement to the sales floor. If you are a baseball fan, picture what the stadium would be like when Barry Bonds steps up to the plate. How about Michael Jordan in basketball? The stadium or arena becomes electric and everyone is looking to see greatness happen right before their eyes. They bring fans into the seat and sell out stadiums. Their team-mates see this and it raises their level of play to achieve the same success.

Unfortunately not everyone can be a super star. That is just fact. There are some who will put in just as much time training as a super star and never reach that level of success. To think otherwise would be foolish. However, you can learn a thing or two from them and better yourself to achieve greater success. I may never be as smooth or well liked as Ty is. He is in another league when it comes to sales. I can assure you that I will try my best to get there someday and utilize what he showed me to the best of my abilities. I have found a much greater success in my career because I implemented and maintained what I learned from him. The benefits I have received from knowing him are still ongoing. I am honored to be the Scottie Pippin of the team. He was a pretty good player and won many championships too.

In closing this chapter I ask you reflect on your career to this point. Who impacted you in such a powerful way? Have you reached the full potential of everything they taught you? If not, I advise you to rethink those memories and moments of greatness and implement them into your sales arsenal. Learn from them and squeeze out every bit of success you find. Do not squander these treasures given to you or hide them. They do no good buried deep within. Let them out and share the wealth with your customers.

Chapter 3

Understanding the Modern-Day Customer

The world has changed drastically over the years and with it so has the customer. The advances in technology have been able to give the customer so much more information. There is good information that educates the customer and makes them more aware of what they are shopping for. Then there is misinformation that confuses the customers and contradicts the sound information. What you find is a customer who is often overloaded with too much information. This can leave the modern-day customer confused, on edge and guarded. It is hard for them to separate facts from fiction without the proper guidance and knowledge. They simply want to find someone they can trust. Someone who can guide them through the sale knowing they have their best interest in mind. Gaining trust is the first thing the modern-day customer desires.

Now take a moment and think about the pressures of modern-day life. Our society demands so much and as they say, "life can be very difficult." It has left a generation of pleasure seekers who are looking for something to relieve the pressures of modern-day life. They find relief through things like television, sporting events, video games and social functions. Whatever it may be, they are looking for an escape from whatever may be stressing them. The modern-day customer simply wants to be entertained.

This is an area in which many sales professionals lack the proper training and skills in order to be successful with the modern-day customer. Facts and product knowledge will only get you so far with today's customer. Putting on a good show while you are selling your customer is one of the key ingredients that is missing from many sales presentations today. This is one of those little treasures I spoke about that will revolutionize your sales performance and success.

Putting on a good show is easier said than done. Because you are the director of your show it is up to you to find out what will work for you. In chapter 5 I will give you the road map of ways to put on a fabulous show for your customers. Right now we need to focus on who the modern-day customer is and how to understand them better.

There are many types of customers who walk through your doors every day. Each one is different. They all have certain needs and desires that need to be met. Meeting these needs will allow you the chance to build trust, make a sale and have a customer for life. To simplify things I like to break every customer down into four basic customer types. They are as follows: Demanding, Analytical, Guarded and Simple Minded. Every customer you meet can be sifted into one of these four categories. I want to break down each of these four customer types in greater detail. As we discuss each customer type we will explore ways to give them the proper service they desire. Knowing how to handle each customer type will give you a greater opportunity for success.

Many of you have taken training courses on the four basic personality types. Some may use animal names such as lion, monkey, turtle and giraffe. Others may use analytical, amiable, expressive and dominant. This is all very important information to learn and will help you. The problem is that the modern-day customer changes constantly based on the experiences they are going through in life. You as a sales professional have the ability to create whichever customer type you desire no matter how they arrived in your store. Give the customer bad service and you will probably create a demanding or guarded customer. If you do not know your product well then they probably will have a few questions and become analytical. Finally give them an amazing experience filled with passion and energy and you will most certainly create a simple minded customer. Follow along as we explore each customer type and let it soak in.

What better way to start than focusing on the demanding customer. These customers can be very difficult to sell if not understood. They can be intimidating and have caused fear in many sales associates. Handle them incorrectly and your chance of survival is slim. It is our negative experiences with demanding customers that create a fear within us when selling them. Before you know it you are selling with your guard up, you forget that this is your customer and your goal is to make a sale. In order to find success you must understand the demanding customer better to help you overcome your fear.

I often like to take life experiences and translate them to the sales floor. Did you know that the demanding customer is just like a shark? What would you think about swimming with sharks? I think it must be terrifying to go into the water with a creature that has the ability to cause you serious pain or even death. It is this fear that the demanding customer has created within us. We see a news report of shark attacks as well as movies like *Jaws* and suddenly every shark becomes a danger to us. It becomes instinct that swimming with sharks would be very dangerous. This is often how we look at selling a demanding customer.

As research has been done on sharks we now see that these creatures have been misunderstood. If we treat them with respect and know how to handle them the fear and danger disappears. I am sure you have watched the research divers who will go swimming with the sharks. We all watch with great interest as we expect to see a negative outcome. We watch in amazement as the research diver blends right into the shark's environment. How were they able to do it? The answer is simple. He took the time to understand the sharks and treated them with respect.

Respect is the first skill needed to find success with a

demanding customer. If they feel respected then they will allow you to enter their environment. The best way to show a demanding customer respect is to let them feel like they are in control. Do not try to lead them or guide them in a direction they do not want to go. What would happen if you tried to steer a shark in a direction it did not want to go? You would probably get bitten. When a demanding customer does not feel in control you will most certainly see the negative results that follow. So make sure to respect your demanding customer by letting them lead you in the sale. If at some point you feel uncomfortable where they are taking you do not be afraid to "zap them truth", then they will know that you also have the power to defend yourself. Most of the time you will find that the demanding customer will lead you without resistance straight to the close.

Now that you have replaced fear with respect you will be able to find a greater success with the demanding customer. The next skill needed to find success with a demanding customer is learning how to serve them. Once you learn how to serve them while you are selling then a great transformation begins to take place. Your demanding customer will not have the desire to be negative towards you in any shape or form. This is just like the shark that is fed by the research diver. Once it is established that good things are coming from the diver the shark has no interest in harming him. The shark is conditioned and trained to act this way.

So how do you serve a demanding customer, you may be asking. You feed a demanding customer with kindness and confidence. When you are nice to demanding customers and start stroking their ego it is very hard for them to display those negative reactions. Instead of harming you they would prefer to be fed more good things. Other ways to serve could be even easier. Offer them a cold beverage while they shop or offer to clean and inspect their jewelry for free while they shop. Try these little offerings of service and watch your demanding customer start to treat you with respect.

These skills that you just learned have one main goal. It is to create an obligation within the demanding customer to be nice to you, trust you and buy from you. Creating obligation is not a negative word. It is the key result that you should look for in every customer type. It creates a beautiful word called loyalty. If you build a customer base with trust and loyalty then you will be very successful.

The next customer type you need to understand is the analytical customer. The analytical customer desires one main thing: information. They need to understand everything in order to feel comfortable with their shopping experience. This could be the bridal customer who enters with a folder full of facts and figures or it could be the intellectual who soaks up every bit of information they could possibly acquire. Either way these customers simply want to obtain information.

So what is the best way to sell these customers in order to better meet their needs? The first thing needed is attention, and lots of it. Always make sure you are listening to them very intently. Then reaffirm that you were listening by repeating a portion of what they say. Let them know you understand them before you answer or explain.

As you answer make sure you maintain good eye contact with them assuring them you are confident in what you are saying. Keep your answers simple and to the point. If you talk too much you might open the door for a marathon sale. These customers are not afraid to challenge you or ask the difficult questions. Give them just enough to satisfy their needs.

The next key to selling an analytical customer is to compliment them. Let them know how impressed you are with their knowledge. Make them feel good about their knowledge, and do it quickly. An intellectual customer will not stop questioning until they feel they have been heard or understood. Sometimes I will even let them feel as if they are superior to me in their knowledge. It's like playing possum. If it helps me get to the close quicker or stay alive then I will surrender. Allowing them to feel superior is a way to take the ammunition away from these customers. There is no need to go into battle if you have surrendered. Their ego is stroked and they feel they have conquered as you ring up the sale and send them on their way. Since you have been conquered there is no need for them to battle with you next time because now they are your friend and not your enemy.

The best way to understand an analytical customer is to examine the game of chess. If you have ever played chess you will know it is a game that demands your wits and skill. It takes a tremendous amount of mental energy and patience to be successful. You must bring your A game when selling an analytical customer. One of the keys to finding victory in chess is playing with vision. You must look ahead and anticipate your opponent's future moves as well as your own. If you have good vision you will find great success in playing chess. No matter what move they make you will be prepared to act because you have planned it out with vision in your mind already.

There is one important thing you must remember as you are anticipating your analytical customer's moves. It is that they are often anticipating your moves also. Be careful not to lose sight of this important information as you are strategizing to lead your analytical customer to the close. By utilizing these skills you will find yourself calling check-mate more often with your analytical customers.

The final skill necessary to finding success with an analytical customer is patience. This is an area that I find difficult to display on a regular basis. You must have patience in order to satisfy the analytical customer's needs. These customers will often require an extra amount of time and energy to finally close. Do not take it personally or feel as if you are not being efficient. The analytical customer needs time to process information and make an educated decision. For those of you who do not have patience I encourage you to turn over the sale with an analytical customer. The old saying that half of something is better than nothing definitely rings true here.

We now move along to the most common customer type. It is the guarded customer. These customers come into your store with a wall built up to protect them from any harm. They are often insecure and feel vulnerable or that you will take advantage of them. They may not know much about jewelry which makes them feel insecure. Also, they may have been ripped off in the past or taken advantage of. Many men feel this way because they are out of their element when they enter a jewelry store. Send them to a car or boat store and you will have a totally different customer type. The lack of knowledge and interest in jewelry, mixed with vulnerability, is the perfect blend that creates a guarded customer.

The most famous guarded customer is the, "I am just looking" customer. You just ran full speed ahead into an invisible brick wall. Still stunned you get up off the ground emotionally and let them know to call you if they see anything they like. Then you retreat to your desk until you get the courage to try again. This can be very funny to watch when it happens to other sales associates. It is not that funny when it happens to you. When they come back in retreat I always tell them to sit back and relax a moment. Sometimes I will show them how it is done properly. Other times I will advise them how to approach them the next time and it usually works.

It is clear that the first key to finding success with the guarded customer is gaining access behind the wall. Selling the guarded customer is just like dating. Just as with finding success in dating you must catch the guarded customer's eye. This is done by creating a trust that you have their best interest in mind. You can do this by offering service that benefits them. It could be a bottle of water or beverage after coming in from the heat, or coffee if it is cold outside. Let them know you are there to serve them and not just sell them. Serving your guarded customer is the best way to break down the barrier.

Another way to gain access to a guarded customer is to make them smile. I use some great opening lines that are designed to relax the guarded customer. I will discuss these in more detail in a later chapter. Relaxing the guarded customer is vital to gaining their trust. Once a guarded customer shares a smile with you then you know that you have access to begin the sales process.

The next way to find success with the guarded customer is to always be genuine with them. If they sense you are not being genuine and just out for a sale they will distance themselves from you quickly. This is best displayed in watching nature shows. Have you ever watched as an antelope is being stalked by a lion? They take off and do whatever is necessary to get away from the predator. This is how your guarded customer feels if you decide to pounce on them. They are no longer a sale but rather just a piece of meat. In order to give you a better insight I encourage going to shop where you know very little about the product. Now you will become the antelope and you will understand the ways of the guarded customer. This will create some compassion and understanding for these very important customers.

It is also important to make sure that you are completely honest while selling a guarded customer. If you are caught misrepresenting a product or being dishonest, they will withdraw. It is like a turtle retreating into its shell. Once it is in its shell there is no way to get it to come out again unless you leave. If you ever make the mistake of misrepresenting something to a guarded customer it is best to turn over the sale immediately. That customer will not open up to you again. These are the skills necessary to find success with the guarded customer.

Finally we end with the simple minded customer. These are the customers who know you well and with whom a bond of trust has been established. They know that you have their best interest in mind and will offer you little resistance while assisting them. You have earned their respect and they reward you with a loyalty that is unmatched. These customers are the foundation of your success and should be treated more like friends.

Creating a simple minded customer is the ultimate reward you can receive when you give them excellent service and an amazing experience. If you noticed I used the word "creating". A simple minded customer is something that you must create within your customer base. It takes hard work and perseverance to achieve such success. Following the road map I have created for the modern-day sales professional will help you find such success. Make sure you give them an amazing show-like experience that leaves them desiring more. Set yourself apart from the standard mindset of selling. It is when you learn how to serve your customer while selling that beautiful things begin to happen. A transformation takes place within the customer and a loyalty is established that is unmatched.

One of the most important things you should remember is that you have the power to create whatever customer type you desire. If a customer comes in and you give them bad service then you have created a demanding customer. They may have not been demanding when they walked in but bad service helped transform them into something they were not. If you do not know your product well and appear uneducated then you could create any of the other three customer types. It is important to understand that people react to how they are treated. This is a golden nugget of knowledge that will transform your career if you grasp the concept and implement it into your customer's experience.

Hopefully this has opened your eyes to understand the modern-day customer. Being able to recognize who they are will allow you the opportunity to sell them with greater success. It is important to remember that the modern-day customer is always capable of changing customer types and you have to be prepared to sell them properly whatever way they arrive at your store. The goal is to give such amazing customer service that every customer eventually becomes a simple minded customer who trusts you completely. I challenge you to explore this gift of understanding the modern-day customer to its fullest potential. It is a deep well of knowledge that will never run dry.

Chapter 4

Building a Strong Customer Base

Everyone knows that the customer is the life-blood of our stores. Without them we simply would not exist. Owners are constantly trying to bring them into their stores in many ways. It all starts by finding a great location and building a beautiful store. Then they spend vast amounts of money on advertising and buy quality merchandise that is unique to the area. Next they hire the best sales professionals available to give excellent service. The list goes on and on. Everything they do is geared towards achieving success and building a good reputation in the community. They are fully invested in finding success. Building a strong customer base is their main objective. A customer base that is loyal and will shop with them for any of their jewelry needs.

After reading this chapter I encourage you to ask your owner what it was like when they started the company. I am certain you will be surprised at the stories they tell. Things are almost never easy in the beginning. Only the strong will survive. It takes courage and faith to start up a business. When times got tough it was passion and a belief in what they were doing that fueled them though it. I have heard the stories from a few owners and they always sound the same. It was not an easy process but the reward is always great. Every one of them will tell you it was the customer base they built that is now the biggest part of their success.

As sales professionals we should strive to build our own customer base with the same passion and belief in our success. Unfortunately many sales associates are clueless on how to properly build a strong customer base. Many are happy just to close a sale and hope that the customer will come back again. If only they knew just how much income they were throwing away every time they do this. The main purpose of this book is to show you how to build a strong customer base for lasting success. Implementing what you will learn from this chapter should raise your yearly salary by at least $10,000 every year. That is right, I said every year. Often times the increase is greater than you might have anticipated.

If the previous paragraph got you excited that is a good thing. This means you actually want to make more money. The problem is many people desire to make more money but are not willing to do what is necessary to achieve it. It will not be handed to you on a silver platter. You have to work very hard to touch your customers in a special way that will separate you from every other sales associate they see. Everything you read in this book is geared to help you build your customer base.

Every customer that walks through your door presents you with an opportunity: they can become your customer for life. You have a chance to become their personal jeweler. This is the way you must approach every customer in order to be successful. It all starts with the first impression. The moment they meet you will define your future with that customer forever. Were you able to relax them? Did they trust you enough to buy something? Did they leave feeling better than the moment they arrived? In time you will find out how successful you were. You will tell by how many people return to purchase from you that were not ready to purchase on their first trip. If you often have customers leave that do not return, this should tell you that something is wrong and needs to be fixed.

For those of you who do see your customers return and purchase a majority of the time, I congratulate you. You are skilled in the art of selling. You might do very well in sales and make a decent living. The next question I have is what did you do after the sale? Did you send them a thank you card? Did you send them a birthday or anniversary card? Did you fill out a wish-list for future purchases? Did you invite them in for free cleaning and inspection? If not, what makes you think they will feel obligated to come back and ask for you again? You have done nothing but sell them an item for their occasion. That is what you were hired to do. You will not get any extra brownie points for that.

How many times do you see sales associates get frustrated when a customer returns and does not ask for them? It is because they did not create an obligation within the customer to come back and see them again. Creating an obligation is the key if you want to have a loyal customer. I have had customers tell me that they felt they had to come and buy something from me because I sent them a nice Christmas card. Even if they did not need anything at that moment the next time an occasion arose they thought of me first. You must learn to separate yourself from the standard sales associate and stand out to the customer.

To create a customer that is loyal to you there must be something different you can offer them. Did you know that learning how to put on a good show for the customer is an option that is available and that will set you apart? It is important that you put on a show for your customer that will leave them wanting more. To be successful in today's sales world you have to do more than just sell them. In the next few chapters I will walk you through the process of a normal sale and show you how to put on an amazing show that will separate you from the normal sales associate. This is a secret and a treasure that will transform your career forever.

Finally it is important that as you build your customer base you maintain it properly. Make sure you do all the little things needed after the sale that let your customer know you are there for them. Go beyond a normal thank you card. Call them up just to say hello with no sales pitch or agenda. Remember their birthday and anniversary. Shoot them a quick email saying hello.

Invite them in to clean and check their jewelry so they can wear it with confidence. After all they are your advertisement and you should always want their jewelry to look its best. I love using that as a one liner. It is one of my favorites. Touch their lives in a meaningful way and they will reward you with the gift of allowing you to be their personal jeweler.

Chapter 5

Welcome to the Show

So far we have focused on what a sales professional should look like. We have learned to understand the modern-day customer and what it takes to assist them better. All this led to the crux of this book in building a strong customer base. Now is the time to learn how to achieve this ultimate goal. The vision has been given to you and it is a road map for a greater success. Most training sessions give you a beautiful vision and leave you with very few instructions on how to get there. Without a proper map the odds are that you are going to get lost and never find your final destination. It is my desire to give you more than you anticipated and so help you reach your full potential.

In earlier chapters we saw that the modern-day customer is looking for something different. No longer will learning the selling basics set you apart from anyone else. When that happens it is important that you examine yourself in the mirror and find something that is special and different. You need to find something that is new and fresh, something that will give you the upper hand. That is exactly what I decided to do and the results have been amazing. I decided to learn how to be a showman as well as a sales professional. Through trial and error I created a show experience for all my customers. Then I mixed in the sales skills I had learned over the years. My sales took off and never looked back.

Learning how to give my customer a show experience during their visits has transformed me from being a good sales professional to someone who can achieve greatness. Now I want to share this treasure with the sales world and revolutionize today's sales floor experience. Take a moment and think about the top sales professionals you may know. Now picture their success with a new weapon that is state of the art. It would have all the latest technology and they would be unstoppable. I could only imagine how lethal Ty would be with this knowledge. The time has come to turn the tide and bring success back to the sales floor. Actually success has never really left. It has always been there waiting for you to find it.

I want to take a moment and say that it is important not to forget the basic sales training that you have received. It is all still a vital part of your success. It has a purpose and needs to be refreshed frequently. Without it all you have is just a show. My goal is to build upon previous success and show you new heights. So let's get started on our journey to new-found greatness.

Let's begin with what will fuel a great show. It is passion and positive energy. Passion is something that can be created with an intense focus and a desire for success. When you have a vision and a goal of what you want to achieve then passion suddenly appears. It is the energy that you put out that drives the passion into different directions. Positive energy will guide you to greater success. Negative energy will choke out the passion and hinder you from greatness.

In today's world there are so many things that can occur that will allow your passion and energy to escape. It could be a troubled relationship, financial difficulties, illness or even a bad store environment. These things can put holes in your mental fuel tank and before you know it your passion and energy have trickled away. You are left empty and wondering what happened. It is important to check your passion and energy levels frequently and make sure that they do not drop. It is also equally important to find out what things are hindering you from greatness and to repair the damage.

Have you ever witnessed a store that is electric? The atmosphere is filled with positive energy as you walk about. You can't help but be excited and go with the flow. This would be a very happy place to work, wouldn't it? There is one time of year when this wonderful phenomenon takes place in most stores. It is the Christmas season. There is a feeling of excitement, happiness and a joy that is present. What a wonderful time of year. I love Christmas season.

Now fast forward a few weeks after Christmas. Is the store's energy level still the same? Is there the electric atmosphere still present? The answer is almost always NO. What happened? Sales associates allow negative energy to creep in like a cloud. This is probably the best illustration of how negative energy will create those holes in your mental tanks and drain your passion and energy. They are too busy focusing on the possibilities of returns and exchanges. Customers become a burden to many sales associates. Their job no longer seems to be as appealing to them and the joy has vanished. They have allowed negativity to choke the positive environment right out of their store. Why do we let this happen? We could create Christmas season energy all year long if we wanted to. In my store that is what we strive to do.

You will be amazed at the decrease in returns if you maintain a positive environment and energy level. In most cases we sell up our customers who come in to return and we are better off than we were before. If we do have a return we do it with joy and thank them for giving us the opportunity to be their jeweler. This will leave a long-lasting positive impression on your customer. They will actually feel guilty that they are returning something. You, my friend, have just created an obligation for them to shop with you next time they need something.

The other major benefit of selling with passion and energy is that it will build your customer base rapidly. I have witnessed this first-hand through my own sales experience. The bottom line is that people like to be around someone who makes them feel good. By selling with passion and energy you will actually fill up their emotional fuel tanks. Think about that for a moment. It is a gift that you are giving to the customer because they are leaving your store fuller than when they arrived. You are no longer just selling your customer. You are impacting their lives in a positive way. When you receive a free gift you feel obligated to return the kindness with loyalty.

It is so important to have energy in your store all year long. Who says that March or September have to be low-volume months? People will buy according to the environment you create. This can all happen when one person decides to make a difference. It only takes one sales professional to implement this passion and energy in a store. Like a spark it can ignite your store. Others will see your success and follow. In the past it was the manager's job to create such an environment. Times have changed and it is up to you to raise the level of energy in your store. Now is the time for true sales professionals to shine.

Now that we see the importance of creating a positive work environment let's start focusing on the sales presentation in more detail. As usual it all starts in the beginning. The greeting is the start of your show. It will define the path and direction of your whole sale. Have you ever watched a show or movie that started out really slow? It is usually a good indicator that the whole movie will be much of the same. Even if it actually gets any better it is still hard to get back into the movie because of the slow beginning. Customers feel the same way about the way they are greeted.

Now let's look at an alternate scenario. How about the movie that starts out with a bang? From the moment it begins you are caught up in the action. When the opening scene slows down you are totally involved and left with a desire to see more. This is usually a good indicator that the movie will be great. Even if it never reaches the same level of excitement again, the great opening scene has captured the audience and they are now enthralled.

Any smart individual could tell you that the second scenario will lead to a greater success. If this is the case then you must examine yourself and see how your greeting is performed. Is it full of enthusiasm? Are you hustling with a sense of urgency and excited to greet your customer? Are you using good eye contact and the proper tone in your voice? Most importantly, is there a big fun smile on your face? These are the keys to a great first impression.

What I witness in many stores is the opposite of the things I spoke of above. There is one negative situation I despise the most. I will see a sales associate who will size up a customer when they walk through the door. If they don't fit the criteria for a big sale they go into what I call the death stare. This is when they turn and face the computer screen and stare hoping someone else will greet them. This can go on forever if no one else greets them. They are committed to looking busy or ignoring the customer. This is usually the case with the sales associate who is in last place in sales. They live and die by the big sale. They will never have a loyal customer base.

Other things I witness are less obvious but just as lethal to a poor opening experience. Have you witnessed someone who greets with very little enthusiasm? Their posture is horrible, there is no eye contact and the tone in their voice makes the customer feel as if they are a burden. We all know what a poor greeting looks like. If we are not careful to examine ourselves in the mirror daily we can become like this without even knowing it. One day you will decide to look and examine yourself and what you find is very unattractive. This would be the time for an extreme greeting makeover. You can do this in every aspect of your sales presentation.

So it is clear that greeting with passion and energy is very important to starting out your sale. This is easy to do when a high-end car pulls into the parking lot or someone who appears to have money walks through your door. The question is, can you generate the same passion and enthusiasm for the average-looking customer who walks in with a watch in their hand? Most sales associates walk up with the mindset that this is just going to be a watch battery replacement. I walk up with the mindset that this is my new customer and they are going to be important to my success. Maybe not right now but eventually it will pay off through referrals or purchases of their own.

In order to be successful you must learn to treat every single customer the same way. Repair customers are not to be treated with any less enthusiasm than a bridal customer. If you treat that repair customer with passion and enthusiasm they will remember you the next time they are ready to purchase something else. They may even tell a friend or co-worker how well you treated them and this will open up an avenue that otherwise would not have existed. In order to be great you must be willing to aim for perfection in the little things just as in the big things.

Earlier I spoke about the associate walking up to the watch customer with a certain mindset. Since we are learning about the greeting I will share with you a little secret of mine that I use to start my day off right. I show up about 15-30 minutes early every day and prepare my mind for success. Preparing your mind for success gives you a huge advantage. Without the proper mindset and self-examination your efforts will be less fruitful. It is in these moments that I can focus on the day at hand. I will force myself to block out all outside influences that could hinder my performance. This allows me to start off my day on the sales floor with positive energy and passion.

The benefits of greeting with a sense of urgency and excitement will set the tone for your sale. It relaxes the customer and lets them know that you are there to serve them, rather than sell them. Make sure you offer a cold drink before you get started. Offer to clean and inspect their jewelry for free before you start. This allows them time to warm up and creates that wonderful word: obligation. How could they not open up to you after you have given them such great service? Your odds just went way up.

These things all lead to building trust. Once your customers trust you then your sales will flow more smoothly. It opens the door for an opportunity to win them over for life. However, this is just the beginning of your sale. It is how you handle the rest of your sale that will determine whether or not you make the sale and gain a customer for life. Let's just take a brief moment and cherish the fact that you are now ready to greet your customer in a way that will set the tone for success in your career.

Chapter 6

Breaking Down the Barrier

We closed the last chapter by focusing on building a lasting trust with each customer. The fact is that most new customers who enter your store simply do not trust you. Don't take it personally. The way the world is today teaches us to be cautious and assume the worst from people. There was a time when people could leave their doors unlocked and go about their daily lives without fear of others taking advantage of them. Those were wonderful times. However, the greed and self-indulgence of today's society has forced people to put up walls and barriers to protect them from being harmed. The sad truth is that the actions of a few bad apples have ruined it for everyone.

Your job as a sales professional is to get past these walls and barriers in order to find long-term success. There are so many sales associates who focus on closing the immediate sale and forget about the big picture of creating future sales with their customer. It is like being so focused on one cupcake that you forget about the other eleven that are also there to be enjoyed. There is so much more success out there to be enjoyed if you can see the big picture. Why would you only settle for one sale when you could have so many others to go along with it down the road?

The whole sales process is about finding ways to reach your customer beyond the walls and barriers in place. Every phase of your sale may have different obstacles but if you stay the course your reward will be a lifelong customer. In this chapter we will focus on doing just that. It is the post-greeting where you will need to discover valuable information to lead you to a successful sale. This is a part of the sale where it is most important to reach your customer beyond their walls of doubt and fear. Let me take you beyond the common knowledge of questioning and help you explore a new world of customer service.

Many of you have learned how to ask open-ended questions to draw out the customer. It is the basic training on who, what, where, when and why. These are all very important in order to get to the facts that you need to be successful. However, there is a special ingredient that I often see missing on today's sales floor. That ingredient is a genuine interest for the well-being of your customer. It is at this moment I will ask you to examine your mindset. Are you doing things just to make a sale? If so, that is all you are going to get: just a sale. It is more important to have a mindset of how you can better serve the customer. Make sure they leave feeling good about themselves and their experience.

After giving a wonderful greeting there are a couple of simple statements that I recommend you use to show your customer your genuine interest in serving them. I will say, "In order to make sure that I meet all your needs there are a few questions I would like to ask you. I want to make sure you are given the best service possible." If the customer is still a little guarded this statement will reassure them that you are there to serve them rather than just sell them. It is what I call a door opener. It is much easier to walk through a door that has been opened rather than charge it while it is closed.

Have you ever watched a sales associate go straight in for the kill right after their greeting? Their customer was just getting relaxed and out of nowhere they are bombarded with question upon question. How do you think the customer feels at this point? Do you think that you just built the trust you needed for long-lasting success? I think not. In fact the customer is probably even more cautious than they were before. At this point they are most likely invested and will answer your questions. However, this will not be a lifelong customer who will be loyal to you.

Hopefully you see that it is very important to reassure the

37

customer of your intentions to serve them before you begin to ask the important questions. This is an important moment in building a lasting trust. Information will begin to flow freely if the customer feels respected and protected. I want you to remember these two words: respected and protected. These are two powerful words that eliminate fear in customers. Once fear is gone your job will be a lot easier. In order to put on a successful show your customer must feel respected and protected.

So now you have greeted your customer with passion and energy. You have allowed them time to understand that you are there to serve them rather than sell them. Now is the time to find out the important information to give your customer the most efficient sales presentation possible. The key at this stage is to get to the point and stay focused on your customer's needs. You need to find out the basics. Who are they here to shop for? What is the occasion that they are shopping for? When is the occasion going to take place? Finally what gift ideas have they in mind for the person they are shopping for?

By focusing on these four questions you can trim down the amount of time you spend on your sales presentation. This will allow you to be more effective and efficient throughout your sale. Straying from these questions will lead you to unproductive talk and will waste time. The more you talk the less you will listen. The less you listen the greater the risk of losing your customer. For those of you who tend to talk too much, this section is very important. You need to pay attention to it and apply these principles.

There is one question I suggest that you focus on the most. It is the importance of knowing the specific time of the occasion. Why is this question so vital to your success? It will allow you to understand which avenue to take in closing your sale. If the occasion is within 48 hours then you need to make sure that you sell this customer something before they leave. The odds of them returning go down drastically if they are allowed to leave without purchasing or committing to an item. They will go and shop elsewhere if you are unable to reach them and satisfy their needs.

When you allow your customers to go shop elsewhere you allow yourself to be a victim of circumstances. They could find an item that might appeal to them more. They could find an item that appears to be a better price to them. Last but not least they could simply change their mind on buying jewelry altogether. There are too many avenues left open for your sale to run away.

Another important thing to remember is that most customers already have an idea of what they want to shop for when they arrive. Very rarely do they ever go shopping without a game plan. Simply ask your customer, "What gift idea did you have in mind for this occasion?" Usually they will be more than willing to share with you exactly what they want. In many cases they are relieved that you got straight to the point and did not waste their time. Asking the right questions will make a big impact on your career and your presentation.

Sometimes the customer may truly have no idea what gift they should be looking for. It is times like these a wish-list could make things easier for everyone. Let's assume there is no wish-list. It is now up to you to be a true sales professional and advise them properly. The first option that will help you will be to look at the customer's buying history at your store. This will allow you to see what types of items they have liked in the past. Then you will be able to suggest items that will match previously purchased gifts. Then look for matching items to suggest. Remind them that most people like their jewelry to match. This also keeps you from duplicating or selling items that are similar to what was previously purchased.

So what about the customer who has never shopped at your store before and has no idea of what they want? These are the customers you must win over to build a stronger customer base. It is important to take some extra time with these customers. Get to know them a little before you sell them. Find out what they do for a living. How long they have lived in the area. Once you have gained this valuable information it is up to you to make an educated suggestion as to what might be a successful gift. Many customers will listen to your suggestions because you have shown them that you are a professional. They will also be somewhat relieved because if for some reason the gift is not a winner then it is now your fault and not theirs.

Earlier we spoke about the wall that many customers have in place to protect themselves. These walls are often created by fear and insecurity. Fear can be a powerful force if you allow it to be. Many customers are unaware at how captive they are to the power of fear. You must learn to recognize when fear is present and face it for them. Once they see that you have helped them overcome their fear then you will be held in high regard. Having the knowledge to set your customer free from fear is a gift and a powerful sales weapon.

In dealing with many customers I have found two common fears. The first is being taken advantage of or cheated. The second is picking out the wrong item and having their gift rejected. These fears are even more intensified in men because many men hate shopping altogether. Helping them conquer these fears will allow them to trust you and build a lasting bond with you. This will allow you to obtain the important information that is necessary before you open up the jewelry case. Later in chapter 12 I will share with you some secrets that have made me very successful with bridal customers. Make sure you remember to look for it. You will not want to miss this.

Chapter 7

Managing Your Sales Presentation

What do you think is one of the biggest problems on the sales floor today? It could be a lack of passion and energy, poor customer service, or a lack of product knowledge. The list could go on and on, as many people come up short in different areas. The items listed above will lead to a sales associate getting terminated or quitting and throwing in the towel. I want to address the main issue that I see in good sales professionals who are doing the right things and striving for success. They simply lack the ability to manage their sales presentation.

They key to managing your sales presentation is summed up in one main concept. It is your ability to manage your time wisely and meet your customers' needs. Mastering this will allow you more time to be successful and productive. As we focus on this I would like to share with you some common pitfalls that many sales associates fail to see. These pitfalls will hinder you from having a well-managed sales presentation. Once you fall into a pit it can be very difficult to escape and move on. It is my hope that this knowledge will enable you to see these traps before it is too late in your sales presentation. The sad thing is that many times we have no clue of the danger that lies ahead.

As we move along we will examine three sales characters that I have created. Each one will expose a poorly managed sales presentation. The first will be the look-at-me sales associate. The second will be the lousy fisherman associate. The third will be the heart transplant sales associate. All three of these characters will have one common thread. The focus is on themselves and not their customers' needs. They will be very unproductive and waste massive amounts of time. Their sales presentations always become marathons.

Have you ever witnessed a sales associate whose sales presentations always become a marathon? It is very painful to watch. By the end of the sale the customer as well as the sales associate appear to be exhausted. That is if you even make it to the end of the sale presentation. Many customers will find a way to excuse themselves from a marathon sales presentation. They do this with a multitude of excuses and reasons why they need to leave. The sales associate's inability to meet the customer's needs leaves them guessing for answers to try and sell their customer. This is a classic case of not managing your sales presentation very well.

What causes such an event to occur? There are a few things that allow a sales presentation to become a marathon. The first is the inability to truly listen to their customer. They are so focused on talking and selling that they forget to let their customer speak. Everyone should know that a successful sales professional will listen more than they speak. Do you know what happens when you speak more than you listen? You steal the show from the customer. The sale becomes more about you rather than your customer. You have become the classic look-at-me sales associate.

To watch a look-at-me sales associate is to witness a very twisted thing. Part of you is upset while the other part is laughing inside because they just never seem to get it. They get so wrapped up in sharing their knowledge and skills that they deceive themselves into thinking they are doing well. After the customer has heard enough they will always find a way to remove themselves. At this point they would rather stick a pencil in their ear than have to listen to this sales associate another moment. What happens next is the ironic part. The sales associate comes over with a prideful look, very confident that the customer will be back. After all, how could they not come back after such a display of knowledge and skill? The truth is the customer will use that information and go somewhere else to find a sales associate who truly cares about them and their needs. The look-at-me sales associate can never understand why their customers often do not return.

Take a moment and think about the people you have worked with over the years. Can you think of a look-at-me sales associate that you have worked with? I am sure a few names probably came to mind. Now think of the times that you or someone else has tried to help that sales associate. Did they ever change or overcome their need to show off? In most cases they probably never changed. Unfortunately these are the hardest sales associates to repair and get on the right path to success. No one can change them but themselves. You can point things out over and over but they never really see that they themselves are the problem. It is because they are incapable of looking in the mirror to examine the problems. Please do not ever become a look-at-me sales associate.

Did you know that selling is a lot like fishing? If you have the right equipment, the proper bait and the right conditions it can be fun and exciting. An experienced fisherman always brings in a good catch and makes it look so easy. They know exactly what to do to find success. They always know exactly where the hot fishing spots are. Some of it they learn by trial and error, but often they take advice from other successful fishermen. Over the years they master their skill and become quite successful. This is a lot like a very successful sales professional.

On the other hand we have all witnessed the lousy fisherman at some point in our career. They have no idea of what it takes to find success. They simply show up with the wrong equipment with very little clue of what bait to use in order to successfully catch a fish. They do not know where to go so they just throw it out there and wait for a fish. After waiting for hours they decide to pull up their line only to find the bait was taken off long ago. They have just wasted their time waiting for something that was never going to happen. If only they had known there was never any bait left on the hook. So what do they do next? They throw it out again and the pattern repeats itself. Every once in a while they might get lucky but they never really bring in the big haul of fish.

Young sales associates are often viewed this way and that is normal. Only through trial and error will you learn to find success. However, it would be easier if you had someone to teach you the important fundamentals of selling, wouldn't it? You will eventually get there but how well you listen to other sales professionals will determine how quickly you get there. It is the older sales associate that has been around a while and is still a lousy fisherman that I want to focus on. There is no excuse why you should be wasting time and usually be coming up empty. Why would you want to continue on this way? Wouldn't you like to be successful and have a lot of fun? It does not make any sense to go about things the same old way. Open up your eyes and try something new that works.

Our customers are so important to our success. They are the heart of our business. Without them we would not exist. Imagine what your body would do if you were to take away the heart. It would not function at all and you would cease to exist on this earth. Therefore it is very important to take care of your heart and make sure it is well and functioning. I think it is safe to say that we all value our heart and appreciate the job it does to keep us alive. We as sales professionals should also value our customers this way and make giving them excellent service a priority.

I have a question that will seem very stupid. Would you ever jeopardize or harm your heart knowing that it gives you life? Of course you wouldn't. So why would you ever treat your customer poorly or not make them your top priority? Ignoring them so you can finish typing in a repair is like tending to a cut on your finger while your heart is stopping. Don't be a fool. Tend to your heart first and then fix your finger. That is common sense. You would be amazed at how many people try to fix insignificant areas while they ignore their customer. You have just met the heart transplant sales associate.

These sales associates do not understand the value of their customers. They are constantly trying to substitute the customer for other things that are not as important. It could be a phone call, a special order, training lesson, or keying in a repair. The list could go on forever. All these things are important and need to be done but please get your priorities in order. When your customer arrives everything else should go away as you focus entirely on meeting your customer's needs first. You can always go back and finish up whatever you were doing later.

If you know anyone who fits any of these three sales associate types I encourage you to have them read this book or come and attend my training seminars. Maybe their eyes will be opened when a bright light is shined their way. Understanding what not to do is part of the way to properly manage your sales presentation. There are other ways of simplifying your sales presentation that you also need to be aware of. So let's get back to time management and how to shorten your sales presentation.

The next major area I suggest we look at is the ability to cut out the fat in your sales presentation. You want your sales presentation to be lean and healthy. Just like meat a little fat can add some flavor. However, I see way too much fat in today's sales presentations. Have you ever seen a piece of meat loaded with fat? It can be quite unpleasant and downright disgusting. Also, it would be quite unhealthy if you ate it constantly.

There are some things to look for that can create a lot of fat in your sales presentation. They are overselling, useless knowledge and unproductive chatter. These three things can sum up a lot of fat in your sales presentation. Learning to monitor these things will help you become more efficient and productive.

How do you minimize these things from happening? By asking the right questions and determining the proper needs. If you ask the customer what type of ring they have in mind. They might say that they really like the Tacori rings. If that is the case wouldn't you be overselling if you started trying to show them any style until you got to the Tacori rings? You just eliminated a lot of wasted time. Let's say the customer took you down a different path and said they were not sure yet. Try following it up with this question. Can you describe what you see as the perfect ring for you? Many times they will open up and share that they want a low-set mounting with a round center diamond and filigree pave side diamonds. Or they might want a plain mounting with a wider band. Whatever the answer maybe you can narrow down the selection and guide them to the perfect ring without wasting a lot of time.

Think of your sale as a drive to a specific destination. The destination is the close and final sale. These questions are like a map and you have to be prepared to take whatever directions the customer gives you. Whenever I ask a question I see it like a fork in the road. I could go left or right depending on what direction the customer gives me. The key is that I am prepared to go whichever direction I am led. Many sales associates make up their mind which way they want the customer to go and try to lead them that way. You can run into a big problem if the customer does not want to go that way. It is now a battle of wills and can be a long and lengthy process.

Another way to cut out the fat in your sales presentation is to not take the story bait. This is a very common road block for sale associates. A customer will share a story or an experience with you that sounds really impressive. It is almost like throwing bait out to catch you and waste time if you handle it incorrectly. The proper way to handle this is to acknowledge, motivate and move on. Often time we do the opposite. It is natural to want to follow up a neat story with a story of your own. Sometimes it is just to share and other times it done to one-up the customer's story. Either way it is the customer's show and you are stealing it by sharing your own story. Let me illustrate this better for you.

Your customer shares with you that they just got back from a trip to the Bahamas and says it was wonderful. The proper response could be something like this: "That is awesome. I hear the Bahamas are beautiful. I bet you and the family had a blast. I am so happy for you. You deserved it." Then move on. What normally happens is that we follow up with something like this: "That is great. I have been to the Bahamas many times. Did you get a chance to swim with the dolphins? We did and it was awesome. Let me tell you about it." If you have not been to the Bahamas you might say, "That is great. We went to Hawaii earlier this year. Let me tell you about our trip." Now you have a battle of stories that serves no purpose in the sale whatsoever. You took the story bait and with it lots of precious time.

It is my desire that something you have read in this chapter will help you manage your presentation more effectively. Remember that managing your time wisely is the key to a leaner and more effective sale. There is so much out there to learn and apply that it can seem overwhelming at times. We are at the half-way point of the book and I feel like we have covered so much already. Make sure that you revisit the areas that spoke the most to you and examine yourself in the mirror often. This way you will maintain the success that is ahead for you.

Chapter 8

Effective Closing

Let's take a moment and recap our sales presentation thus far. We greeted the customer with passion and energy. Then we established a trust by showing the customer our intention to serve them rather than sell them. Next we uncovered the key desires of the customer by asking them the proper questions and listening. We then followed this up by managing our sales presentation well, cutting out the fat and staying focused on the sale at hand. All this led us to the mountain top of closing the sale. This is the ultimate destination we desire to reach in making a sale.

Closing is often perceived as being the most difficult part of the sales presentation by many sales associates. In fact many sales associates do not even know how to properly close a sale. This is because most of the sales training on closing today is not as effective as it should be. We have been taught to start closing at the beginning of the sale and start trying many ways of closing until one works. Fishing for the close can be tiresome work. We are also shown how to overcome all kinds of objections during our marathon sales. This can work sometimes, but is it really necessary? What if I told you there was a better way to close the sale? That many of the objections that you face are unnecessary. What if I told you that closing could be the easiest part of your sale? I am here to share with you that there is a way to make closing easy. Follow me for a moment as I share a little insight with you.

After many years of selling I often found myself exhausted and burnt out. In order to maintain my success I constantly had to recharge my sales batteries. Selling had become a grind and had lost its luster for me. I just knew there had to be a better way to find success out there. So I decided to use my faith and turn to God for the answers. I asked for new wisdom and an understanding that would set me apart from the rest of the sales world. What I received are the blessings you have read thus far. I thank you heavenly father for your kindness and blessings.

The road map that has been laid before you will lead you to a greater success. You will find that closing will become smoother and painless. Your customer will be more receptive to committing to the purchase. In fact many customers will desire for you to ask for the sale when you meet their needs properly. The customer will become comfortable and confident enough to jump right in when the opportunity presents itself. It is kind of like sky diving. With the proper equipment and a good instructor sky diving can be exhilarating and refreshing. The feeling of accomplishment is great once you decide to overcome your natural fear.

It is up to you to give your customer the confidence they need as their instructor through the sales process. Could you imagine going sky diving with a lousy instructor? What if they appeared just as nervous as you when you headed up into the sky? What if you observed that the equipment that was given to you was old and fragile? Or if when your instructor was packing your parachute they did not seem to know exactly what they were doing? Can you imagine this instructor asking you to jump with them and putting your life in their hands? There is no way possible that anyone would feel comfortable jumping with an instructor like this.

As a sales professional you have to earn the confidence and trust of your customer to jump into the close. Otherwise you are going to meet strong resistance in the form of major objections. The customer will not allow you to lead them into the unknown because they simply do not trust your ability as their instructor. Make sure you give your customer the proper confidence needed to decide to jump into the close with you. This analogy applies mostly to the first-time customer who has never shopped with you before. Once you have proven yourself as a reliable sales professional the customer will be willing to jump with you again and again. It is always the first jump that is hardest, as they overcome their fear.

There is one thing that I want to make very clear as we move along in closing. As you guide your customer during the close there may still be some minor hesitation even if you have done everything correctly. This is very similar to the first-time sky diver needing a little extra reassurance before the jump. Some people call this objection but in reality it is just reassurance they are looking for. There is a major difference between objection and reassurance. Your customers are looking to you as the professional to reassure them that everything will be ok. Make sure that you give them the proper reassurance they need.

Let's take a look at a common reassurance question that a customer may have before taking the jump with you. "Is this the best price you can do?" The customer really wants reassurance that they are not paying too much. They are letting you know that they have found the item they desire and are ready to purchase. A confident sales associate will reassure them and close the sale. If there is any hesitation or lack of confidence in your answer then you have become the unconfident instructor. The customer will not be ready to make the jump with you.

Confidence is the key to reassuring your customer. You do this with good eye contact and a smile as you are reassuring your customer. Let them know that they are receiving excellent quality at great value. Keep it simple and to the point. Make sure you do not oversell the reassurance as this too can be a sign of weakness and uncertainty. If you have established trust with your customer they will usually go along with your assessment and advice because you are the professional.

Another reassurance statement you might hear is, "I really like this one but I am just not sure it is the one." How many times do you see a sales associate miss this reassurance opportunity? Instead of reassuring and closing they open the door of doubt by allowing the customer to continue questioning themselves. Just like the hesitant sky diver this is a great moment for you to reassure them as their instructor that everything is going to be ok. Look them in the eye and let them know that they have made the right decision and that you are excited that they found the perfect item.

The examples could go on and on but the key is confidence. If you are confident in your closing then wonderful things will happen. The problem we find in closing is that many sales associates lack the proper confidence to be successful. Without confidence you will find yourself dancing around objection after objection. This creates a marathon close and often your customer will quit somewhere during the process and ask for your business card so they can try to find the confidence on their own. Many times they will go elsewhere and find a sales associate who will give them the confidence they need to purchase. All your hard work that laid the foundation of the sale is lost because you lacked the confidence to close your customer. This is a common scenario that does not have to happen.

The next key to becoming a successful closer is using your confidence to overcome fear. It is fear that causes many sales associates to lack confidence when they are closing. We all need to understand that fear can affect us just as it does our customers. Many of us allow fear to master us and control us in ways that make us unproductive. Often we may fear rejection from past negative closing experiences. Many times fear is already present based on who we are and our experiences throughout life. In order to defeat fear you must understand it first.

When you think of fear you may think of darkness or something scary. Have you ever watched a movie that created fear within you? Try walking alone in the darkness after fear has placed its grasp on you. Every little sound you hear is magnified and your mind begins to play tricks on you. Before you know it you are running full speed in a panic with the belief that something bad is about to happen or that someone is after you. Even if you had a flashlight to see it would do little to calm the fear that is running rampant within you. I often think of the flashlight as truth. Even though you have knowledge of the truth all is lost in the moment that fear captures you.

This is a common illustration of how sales associates approach a close. They lose all sense of truth and confidence because the fear that controls them is pulling the strings. Like a puppet they are at the mercy of their fear. If only they had not watched that movie. The walk home in the dark would have been fine with the proper light provided. The scary movie is what we create by bad past experiences and failures. We relive them over and over in our minds and buy into the concept that this is the way it is going to be all the time. The key to overcoming fear is exposing it with truth and then moving on. Do not watch the scary movies of failure within your mind and buy into the craziness it brings you to later.

Another way to master fear is by finding strength in numbers. That walk home in the dark after watching the scary movie would be a lot easier if you had a friend with you. Guess what, at this point of the sale your customer should already be your friend. Remember that they are just as scared as you are because they too have watched scary movies in their lives. Learn to find comfort by knowing that your customer is your friend and that they are taking the same walk with you. Together the two of you can overcome fear by exposing it to truth. This is a powerful insight that can be applied in many areas of your lives.

We now know that truth, being the light, and our customer, being our friend, can help us get through the darkness of a close. The question I have for you is, why are you walking in the dark to begin with? Wouldn't it make more sense to walk in daylight? In order to walk in daylight you must first learn to walk through the darkness. Once you have mastered it then you will find yourself walking in daylight on a regular basis. This is another truth that will set you on your way to unlimited success once you have grasped it and applied it.

Life on the sales floor can become so much easier when you take these truths and use them as lights to illuminate your sales career. Before you know it you find a comfort in selling that you have never experienced before. At the beginning of this chapter I asked the question, "What if I told you closing could be the easiest part of your sale?" At that moment I bet many of you wondered if this could really be possible. Now you see that it is possible. It has been proven every year that I sell over a million dollars. People know me for my skills as a closer more than any other skill set that I possess. It is not because I am a super seller or crafty. It is because I took the time to understand my customer, myself and a higher knowledge and wisdom that reveals mysteries. I encourage you to do the same.

Chapter 9

Creating a Lifelong Customer

Along this journey so far you have discovered many new truths and insights that have the potential to change your career forever. It is at this point I would like to turn our attention back to the core issue of building a strong customer base. By now you have given your customer an amazing experience and established a bond of trust that helped you close a sale. This is the point where many sales associates pat themselves on the back and assess their achievements. Like a kid after trick or treating they empty their bag of new successes. What they find is higher sales, commission dollars and congratulations from their peers. My question to you is, why would you want to stop here? Why settle for three pieces of candy when you have the potential to have a bag overflowing with goodies?

When you apply the skills that make you great it is important to maximize your opportunities. Do not be the absent-minded trick or treat kid who is out of candy within 15 minutes and left with nothing. Make sure you keep your success going by adding to your collection of treats. You do this by impacting your customer in a powerful way after the sale. When they are in your store they expect good service, sound information and pro-fessionalism. In return they give you their business and the deal is done. A successful transaction is completed, or is it? What if they received more than they anticipated? Wouldn't that impact them in a powerful way?

You have the ability to solidify a lasting relationship with your customer when you give them more than they were expecting. Many sales associates miss out because they are satisfied with what they have received already. It is kind of like scratching off a lottery ticket. They are hoping to win. A great experience is like scratching off the first number and winning a thousand dollars. What an exciting moment that is! I have actually experienced this myself many years ago. In my excitement I forgot all about the other numbers that had yet to be scratched. I was so happy to have just won $1,000. Then I came to my senses and decided to scratch the other nine numbers. They all had $1,000 winners totaling $10,000. It was more than I had anticipated. Had I just stopped after the first number I would have missed the truth that this was a $10,000 winning ticket.

The true story I just shared with you is exactly what is happening to many sales associates today. They are so happy to win on the first number that they forget to finish the rest and reap a greater reward. It is when you give your customer more than they anticipate that your reward will multiply ten-fold. All it takes is extra time and effort with an intense focus on serving your customers.

The first way of giving more to your customer after the sale is making sure that they receive a hand-written thank you card shortly after the occasion. If the sale was over $2,000 give them a $100 gift certificate for their next purchase as a thank you. Do you think the customer is expecting this? Would they feel obligated to come back and purchase the matching wedding band or jewelry item? You bet they would! You are solidifying the relationship with your customer. They realize that they are more to you than just a one night fling. It becomes clear that you truly care about them and look forward to seeing them again. The thank you card is a powerful tool that will help you build your customer base. I have never understood why sales associates do not take the time to touch their customers' lives in a meaningful way.

The next way to solidify and strengthen a relationship with your customer is to remember them on their birthday, anniversary or on other special occasions. I like to send a really nice card with about a paragraph hand-written note letting them know that I appreciate them and their loyalty. Do you think your customer is expecting this from the sales associate they met with 6 months ago? What a wonderful impact you will create when you remember your customers on their special occasions. This will reaffirm the bond of care and trust that you created with them long ago.

I want to be clear that these things should be done in the right frame of mind and spirit. If you are doing them with the sole purpose of reaping a benefit your efforts will be fruitless. Make sure you do it with the mindset of touching your customers' lives and making them better. Do not expect anything in return, but allow the laws of nature to take effect and you will receive your reward. Making sure that your heart is pure is very important to finding success here. Use the self-examination skills you learned earlier and set your focus on impacting your customers' lives.

Believe it or not there is even more that you can do to touch your customers' lives after the sale. As your customer base grows and you effectively reach them you will become a polarizing figure in the community. When you go to eat dinner or grocery shopping your customers will recognize you because of the great experience you provided. Make sure you recognize them and acknowledge their presence. Greet them with enthusiasm and ask them how they are doing. Make sure your focus is on them and not yourself. Always remember that people like to be remembered and cared about. Those public events that you may not look forward to attending are the perfect setting to see your customers and impact their lives in a positive way yet again.

These are the ways to reach your customers on a deeper level and show them that you truly care about them. There are many other ways to create a lifelong customer that make a difference. Remember that your job is to make each customer's experience as painless as possible. The more comfort you provide the easier things will get. Now that we understand our customers better we must not forget that men and women are very different. Creating comfort for each is very different. I will share with you some insights in creating comfort for men as well as women.

In talking with men about their shopping experience there were two things that remained constant in their thought processes. The first was that they did not like to shop. The second was that they always worried about picking out the wrong item for their spouse. Take away those two things and you my friend will have a lifelong customer with these men. Enter in the power of the wish-list. The wish-list is the greatest tool you can use to give a man comfort in his shopping experience. It makes his shopping experience quick, easy and painless. Unfortunately many sales associates do not use this dynamite to break through the walls of resistance in their male customers. They do not understand the potential they are wasting when they see a wish-list as extra work.

Most of us know how a wish-list works. For the sake of younger sales associates I will explain the basic details. When a woman sees something she really loves it is scanned on her wish-list. The goal is to put a few items on it that give the man a variety to choose from so that he still feels empowered and in control. This helps eliminate any fear or hesitation the man may have because the gift is a guaranteed slam dunk. One thing I stress to ladies is to make sure that they truly love the item they are placing on their wish-list. There is nothing worse than a man purchasing an item from the wish-list and the woman exchanging or returning it. This is a key fact to remember when creating a wish-list for someone.

The next step in making a wish-list successful is to work it properly. A short time before the occasion make sure you remind the customer that there is a wish-list waiting to make things easier for them. If you do not know the male very well it might be better to remind the woman to mention it to her spouse. She will have a greater impact than you will if you are not familiar with him. For the men with whom you have a sales history it should be pretty easy to contact them with a simple reminder. If jewelry is not on the cards for that occasion let them know that you understand and appreciate them. It is important to know that most men are very appreciative that you are helping them. This is another way of serving your customer while selling them.

When assisting ladies the wish-list is not as productive because men are usually not shopping to begin with. If the opportunity presents itself then use it with your female customers also. The best way to impact a female customer after the sale is by offering to service and maintain her treasured jewelry. Give her a friendly reminder call to come in and have her jewelry cleaned and inspected every few months. This lets her know that you care about her as well as her jewelry. The feeling she gets when her jewelry is sparkling and secure is very comforting. Also this will allow her to look around and scan a few items on her wish-list. Again your heart must be in the right place when you offer such a service. Even if she does not shop you win because your advertisement is looking good wherever she goes.

Hopefully you see that impacting your customers after the sale is absolutely critical to finding a greater success. If you implement these skills with a pure heart and a desire to serve your customer you will find many great rewards. This is something we have known in the industry for quite some time but it has not been used effectively. Sales people have not taken the proper time and effort to create such success because it simply takes a lot of hard work. They may begin the process of trying to touch their customer's life but without self-examination they forget what they were supposed to look like. Like a weed that sprouts up, laziness and self-centeredness choke out their efforts. The skills you have learned will help you sustain these important efforts to find greater success.

Chapter 10

The Journey of a Career

Many of you may be wondering what the deepest secrets to my success are. How have I been able to become a million dollar seller year in and year out? I have already shared with you many of the skills that have transformed me into a million dollar seller. Everything you have read thus far is an important ingredient to my success. I effectively use the insights that I have received to set myself apart from everyone else around me. The truth to who I really am may actually surprise you. The truth is that I am actually just an above-average sales associate. What sets me apart to be looked upon as great is what you will find in this chapter.

Did you know that it is possible for a mediocre sales associate to outperform a super seller? I know this to be true because I have witnessed it throughout my career. I have worked with sales associates far more knowledgeable and skilled in the art of selling than me. What made me so much more effective was my ability to connect with the customer and gain their trust. You can have all the skill in the world but if you do not understand people then you are cheating yourself and your customer. This is the missing link in a multitude of super sellers who will now be able to achieve greatness.

The sales world has taught us to be greedy and focus our attention on things that only bring short-term success. Think of how many ways we are taught to trick our customers or manipulate them into something more than they anticipated. You may find success but customers do realize what has happened once they leave. Once you learn to use your sales skills in a way that benefits the customer then you are on your way to finding greater success. It is time for sales associates to get back to being genuine and real with their customers. Today's customer is much smarter than you think. Unless you learn to value your customers you will be chasing after the wind. It will be meaningless.

So far we have journeyed down this new path together and discovered many new things to help us become difference-makers. I know that many of you will use these skills and become great warriors of the sales floor. I predict that you will see an increase of million dollar sellers all over the country because applying this truly will give you an advantage over your competition. When I say your competition I am talking about other sales associates at different locations. Your customer is not your competition. This is a mindset that needs to change and I intend to help in this process. The way sales training has gone over the years teaches us to view our customers as our competition. This is how we got off the path to success and found ourselves in the predicament we are in today.

There is a reason I mention words like journey and path so often. Our lives and careers are a journey and a path. The further you get down the road, the clearer things become. This happens as your destination gets closer, provided you did not lose your way along the journey. The problem with many sales associates is that they have lost their way along their journey and are in desperate need of a road map to help them get back on course. I have gotten off course over the years and by the grace of God found my way back to the right path.

There are some signs that will let you know if you are off course. The first sign is a lack of motivation or passion. When you leave the path to success you will find no filling stations along the way to maintain your levels of passion and energy. Many people call this burn out and that is exactly what it is. The common thing to do is take a vacation and everything will be alright, or will it? Taking time away is very helpful to fill up your emotional energy tank with passion but if you do not fix the holes within your tank you will find yourself on empty again sooner than you think. I have seen great sales associates leave the business because they were never able to figure this out.

The second sign that you are off course is when you find yourself with a lack of compassion or feeling for your customer. When the sale becomes more about the commission dollars or figures then you know that you have lost sight of the true meaning of serving your customer. Like a weed this chokes out any compassion or feelings for your customer's well-being. Now you are known as the predator and not a sales associate. You will find short-term success but always be struggling to achieve greatness.

The final sign I will share with you is the killer of many sales associates. It is when you find yourself being dishonest or deceitful with your customers, as well as your co-workers. When sales associates get lost, and cannot find their way, they often resort to dishonest tactics to help them get by. What they do not realize is that they are driving full-speed right off a cliff. It is only a matter of time before they free fall to the bottom and crash. We have all done it at some point in our career. That sale that should be split but you take the whole sale because the other sales associate is not paying attention. Even worse, that customer you lie to in order to close the sale. These things will catch up with you eventually. For those of you who are on course I encourage you to watch for these signs so you can correct yourself before you get too far off course.

As we move along discussing the journey of your career there are many things you must understand. The first is that you are not alone. There are many others traveling along the same path and it is important to follow those who are ahead of you that are heading in the right direction. Find a mentor or successful sales associate and follow their lead, provided they are doing things the right way. Pace yourself, follow the rules and in the proper time you will reach your destination. The important words to heed are: follow the rules. Your journey is like driving to a destination and there are rules in place to keep everyone safe and traffic flowing freely.

Have you ever driven behind someone who is going way too slow? It can drive you crazy because you know that they are keeping you from getting to your destination in a timely manner. The funny thing is that I often see sales associates following the lead of a super slow mentor. Why would you choose to follow someone who is traveling way under the speed limit set for success? It is important that you find someone to mentor you who is traveling at the right pace. Following someone who is not achieving their full potential can really set you back.

At the other end of the spectrum you must also be careful not to follow someone who is careless and speeding way too fast. This is potentially worse than following someone who is really slow. What happens when you follow a speedster who is not following the rules set for success? Your odds of getting pulled over or in a wreck go way up. Be very selective and careful of whom you choose to follow. The road to success is a very busy road and not everyone is following the rules set for success.

Finally I will end this chapter by sharing a beacon of light that will illuminate your insight and vision. In your journey everything happens for a reason. You may not see it at the time but if you are doing things the right way there is a purpose for everything that happens to you. If something terrible happens in your career it is easy to lose sight of the purpose of your journey. You may take the mindset that life is not fair. Why is this happening to me? What did I do to deserve this? I am here to share with you that there is a divine plan in your journey and sometimes you may not be in control. My advice to you is to have faith that there is a purpose and meaning for everything you go through.

Sometimes people may make a mistake in their journey and there is a price that they must pay. That is just common sense.

However, there are times where you are doing everything right and bad things will happen. It was not anything you did or did not do. This can happen on a personal level, like losing a loved one, or on a professional level. For whatever reason circumstances occur and you are the odd man out bearing the pain and heartache. These are times to try to keep your head up and focus on the future knowing that there is still a destination ahead. This is easier said than done. I know because I have been through this myself.

It was the end of January and my staff and I had just endured a long but successful Christmas season. I had just hired a few new associates before the holiday season and things seemed to be going well. What I was unaware of was that two of the new hires and my long-time assistant were not on the same team at all. They had decided that it was time for me to go and that they would do whatever it took to get rid of me. So they made up a bunch of stories and twisted the truth about certain situations to paint me in a bad light. I did not worry because I knew I had nine years of management experience with this company and no previous write-ups or infractions. I was sure the truth would come out and all would be fine.

I had never been accused of any wrong doing and was confident my record would speak for itself. However, earlier I spoke of circumstances occurring over which you have no control, and this was that moment. What I failed to realize was that this happened three days before the end of January. The company had made all managers sign a contract that if they were not a head manager until January 31st they would forfeit their entire yearly bonus. The circumstances were set. Would this company stand by a nine-year successful manager with no previous history of misconduct? However, if these accusations were true the company could be liable. Besides, they could also save $28,000 by terminating me three days before my eligibility for the bonus. I was just one loyal employee and it was not worth the risk. So, the decision was made to do a one-sided investigation and protect the company even though they knew the accusations were false.

At this moment in my career I was devastated. How could this happen? I trusted these people and had been loyal to this company for so many years. What a bitter pill to swallow. Yet inside I felt a calming voice assuring me that everything would be ok. So I accepted this fate and moved on. Within a week a sales position opening occurred at the local high-end jewelry store. They only had four sales positions so this was a miracle. I applied for the job and was upfront with the owners at the interview about what had transpired. Later I found out that the manager at the time did not want to hire me because of the false allegations, but the owners saw the truth and decided to hire me.

Before I knew it I was off and running. I used the nine years of management experience to manage myself and became an elite sales professional. My lifestyle improved because the hours were much better. We were closed Sundays and Mondays and off by 6pm every night. My life was suddenly much better than it was before. With the extra time I was able to take relationships more seriously and married my beautiful wife Jennifer. My income had increased and success was knocking at my door again with intensity. Now here I am today with some of the freshest insight and vision in sales training, helping others to find success. I can say that my darkest hour led me to the dawn of a new day filled with blessings and greatness.

For anyone who may being going through a challenging time in their career I encourage you to take heart and have faith. Everything truly does happen for a reason. Even if it appears there is no way good can come out of the situation you are in, there is a divine plan set for your life. I always say success is found when you take what is good and make it great. I guess you can also say that in your darkest hour the dawn of a new day of blessings is just ahead. So as you travel on your journey you will do well to understand that these moments of trials can actually be avenues to greatness.

Chapter 11

Unlocking Your Full Potential

In the beginning, a foundation was set for true success. It was laid by our forefathers with trust, integrity, honesty and truth. Upon this foundation was built the selling empire we see today. Somewhere along the way we lost sight of this foundation and began to try new methods of building. We exchanged our truth for a lie and began to build with deception, greed and selfishness. Now as we shed light on our empire we see that there is a problem. The methods we have used to continue building have started to decay and so tarnish our selling empire. What was once a strong fortress is now unstable and crumbling from the inside out. The time has come to tear down this abomination and rebuild on the lasting foundation of truth.

At this point you may be asking yourself if this is a little too dramatic. In response to this I will ask one simple question. Are you truly satisfied with your career? I am not talking about sales dollars, commission or outward appearances. What I am asking is, do you find satisfaction in what you are doing? Are you truly happy within? You would be shocked at how many sales associates answer in the negative to this question. Those industry leaders, top sales associates or mentors you look up to, they too often answer "no". You may be asking, "How is this possible?" They seem to be on top of the world. Surely they would be happy with their accomplishments and achievements. The truth is that no matter how much success they find there will still be a big void within because we got away from the core foundation of truth.

For those of you who have been in the business for many years you know exactly what I am talking about. There was a time when business was conducted with honesty and integrity. As the world changed and evolved greed set in and people began to look for different ways to find success. Leaving the path of truth they ventured out into the unknown to find a quicker route to success. Thus began the era of self-centered sales tactics and trickery to manipulate our customers into buying. For years we have been teaching our sales associates ways of deceit to feed our greed, thinking we will find fulfillment. Now we find ourselves lost in the dark and desperately looking for a light to lead us back to the path of truth.

The moment we decided as an industry that we would stray from the path of truth, darkness began to set in. Like a gentle voice from the dark greed called out with soothing words and promises. The further we strayed, the more it lulled us into the deep sleep of deception. Now a light of truth shines forth calling us to rise up and awake from our slumber. I encourage you to follow this light and allow it to lead you back to the path of truth. If you follow truth your sales career will have purpose and meaning once again. Your customers will begin to trust you and be drawn to you. You will impact their lives in a powerful way when you sell with integrity, honesty and truth. I know this to be true because I have lived it and found my way back to a success full of riches and blessings.

I want to take a moment and mention that there are good sales tactics that can be used to give your customers a great experience. Not all sales tactics are bad or deceiving. Good sales tactics are judged by two main factors: do they benefit the customer, and do you feel good about yourself when using them? If you answer "yes" then these are sales tactics you should use. There is a right way to greet, ask open-ended questions, overcome objections and close the sale. These are not bad sales tactics if used properly. When they are used with trickery or deceit then it is no longer about your customer but all about you. This is where we went wrong.

The consequences of our actions as an industry have caused many to lead careers full of regret and with no fulfillment. Many great sales associates have never reached their full potential. Even worse, we have lost many sales associates who never discovered the potential they had. With this sales revolution that you are going to see taking place there will be many great sales associates who will arise and lead this industry back into greatness. How do I know this? Just take my career as an example. This truth has transformed my career into a yearly million dollar sales associate. To be totally honest there are many more talented sales professionals out there who could achieve so much more with this wisdom and knowledge.

In Store magazine did a poll on stores recently. Did you know that only 6% of sales associates sell over $450,000 yearly? That number astounded me because truthfully I do not consider myself among the elite sales professionals. Yet here I am within the top 1% based on following the simple principal of truth laid down so long ago. I feel it is my calling, and duty, to help these sales associates find a more fulfilling career followed by success. That is why I am actually leaving the sales floor and making sales associates my new customers. My vision and mission is to impact their lives in a powerful way that will help them reach their full potential.

I am going to ask you a question that I want you to think deeply about. What three things do you believe hinder sales associates from finding their true potential? I can almost hear your brain working as you dig deep to find the truth. The answers are: fear, laziness and a lack of knowledge. Every excuse you could find will have one of these three factors at the root of the problem. Let's explore these three pitfalls in greater detail so you can make sure that you reach your full potential.

Earlier in this book I spoke a little about fear and how it affects your customers. Fear is a universal soldier of destruction and no one is safe from its power if they allow it to consume them. Think of how many times you have found fear tormenting you and keeping you from achieving your goal. I will share with you a few experiences from my past that will help illustrate how fear operates. When you take life's moments and use them to better yourself you will be amazed at how the little setbacks can benefit you in a powerful way.

When I was younger I watched a scary movie at a friend's house that greatly affected me. My goal was to walk home from my friend's house that night and my parents would never know that I watched this movie that was forbidden. The problem was that fear had set root within me and I was about to learn a valuable lesson. Before I made it half a block I found myself running back to my friend's house in a panic. I just knew that creature was out there waiting for me. How embarrassing it was to call my dad and beg him to come and pick me up. I had to come clean and let him know that I was just too scared to come home. Because I had let fear master me I had to pay a price for my disobedience.

The first thing I want to point out is that I was doing something I should not have been doing in the first place. When you are doing things the wrong way it opens a door for fear to come in. When this happens fear brings his friend called doubt. Anyone looking from the outside in would say there is nothing to worry about, just head home. However, doubt had convinced me that there was something out there waiting just for me. Against all common sense I took the bait and then entered another friend called shame. When you lose confidence in yourself, and your ability to meet your goal, then shame enters the picture. In the end I wished I had never watched that movie. It created a lot of problems for me. Hopefully you are starting to see a negative pattern of destruction and defeat in this simple story of a disobedient little kid.

I know that story is silly but it illustrates perfectly how the seed of fear can bring you down in a hurry. Now let me share with you a more modern story of fear and how it is trying to keep me from reaching my full potential. This message and insight I am sharing is pretty powerful stuff. It has the potential to bring revival to the sales floor and lead many others to freedom and success. What things do you think fear is doing to try to keep such a message from getting out?

To start with I make a pretty good income as a million dollar sales associate. Doubt says why risk it all to spread a message that might not catch on? What if people do not listen? The advice that I have received from much respected sales trainers has been very discouraging. While appearing to impart wisdom they plant seeds of doubt to hinder me. Watch out for law suits they say. You will go broke at the beginning. Are you sure it's worth it? Take your time and ease into this role. Unless you do this, this and this you are going to fail. It is a good thing that I have faith in myself, my message and my provider. Look at me now.

Did you notice that faith is the key ingredient to overcoming fear? When you have faith in yourself, and your God-given abilities, it overcomes fear. When faith enters it brings along a few friends. First there is hope with a vision of greatness. Hope brings in wisdom and knowledge that later bring success. Then success brings in confidence and so on. Is this starting to make a little more sense? Do you see the difference in what is happening here? Why would you want to continue on living in fear, doubt and shame? This is the secret to unlocking your full potential.

The next thing that hinders you from reaching your full potential is laziness. Earlier in the book I spoke about dependency blindness that has swept across the nation over the years. Many sales associates do not take the time or effort to manage themselves and their abilities. Instead they wait for others to show them the way or do things for them. This is where laziness takes root and it too has friends that it brings along to defeat you. The first friend is complacency who tells you there is no need to work any harder because there is not much more out there to discover. Then complacency invites in deception, who feeds you lies. Before you know it you are in serious trouble and you are not even aware of it.

In order to keep such a thing from happening you must decide who you will invite into your career. I suggest passion and energy. Earlier I mentioned that these are the fuels that drive you to success. When you have passion and energy with you they bring along excitement and fun to the party. Then fun and excitement bring peace and fulfillment. I think you know how it goes from here.

The important thing to notice here is that everything is happening in your mind. It is a choice that you make that leads you to the outcome of your career. Without this knowledge it is easy to be deceived and defeated in such a complex world. That is why the third thing that hinders you from reaching your full potential is a lack of knowledge. There are many faiths out there in the world and most of them stress the importance of knowledge as a key to successful living. I am a Christian and one of the most powerful verses in the Bible is Hosea 4:6: "My people are destroyed from lack of knowledge." There are so many verses in the Bible that point to knowledge being the key to success.

When you have knowledge it invites in a friend called understanding. Then understanding brings in wisdom and insight. The two friends find strength and success following close behind. I think you get the point. Make sure to seek the proper knowledge of what will make you more successful. If you noticed I used the word proper. This is important to point out because there is all manner of knowledge out there and not all of it is good knowledge. Let me illustrate this for you.

Let's say you are in a troubled relationship. You love your spouse so you go looking for knowledge to try to help you understand. On your search for knowledge you find the wrong kind of knowledge. Instead of talking to a consoler you decide to snoop around in your spouse's belongings. The knowledge you find is that they have being seeing someone else and it appears to be getting pretty serious. What type of reaction do you think this knowledge will create? Fear appears because you could be losing your spouse. Doubt enters its two cents that they must not love you. Before you know it you are in a panic. The world is collapsing all around you. I would encourage you to look for the type of knowledge that will be beneficial to your problem and offer you a better solution.

Hopefully this chapter has given you some fresh insight on how to unlock your full potential in your sales career. This information actually applies to many areas of your life but if you apply it towards your sales career you will see a big difference. Understanding these principles can help you live a more fulfilling life and career. I hope you find many blessings that abound over time as this message takes root within your soul.

Chapter 12

Finding Success with Vision and Insight

Over the years the sales industry has become a goal-oriented industry. Sales quotas are set daily, weekly, monthly and yearly as a reminder of where we want to be. This helps us maintain our focus to achieve the ultimate goal set forth by those in charge. These goals and quotas are the temperature gauge of the company that let us know if we are hot or cold. There is a lot of emphasis on maintaining sales goals and quotas. These tools are very effective in keeping everyone aware of their performance as a team and as an individual. As a manager for many years I used sales goals and quotas very successfully to help motivate my staff to perform.

As my career moved on I discovered that goals were just a small part of something much bigger. It was something that nobody really understood or paid much attention to. The truth I discovered was that goals were the descendants of vision and insight. For years we have been focusing on something that was just a small piece of the bigger pie. Goals and quotas are great but I am here to share with you today that there is more out there that is yet to be explored. Today, I would like to teach about the greater purpose of vision and insight. In order to grasp the bigger picture of vision and insight we must first understand where they have been.

As I mentioned earlier these are the parents who gave birth to goals and quotas. Over time they were forgotten because everyone was so focused on the new little ones. My brother and his wife recently had a beautiful little girl named Charis. She is now eight months old and the center of everyone's attention. Every time we go over to visit or baby-sit for them it is all about

Charis. After a while I realized that we never paid much attention to Brett or Christi and their needs. We would show up and play with Charis. Everything she did, no matter how small, was magnified and admired. If she rolled over it was amazing because it was fresh and new. If Brett and Christi rolled over they would not get quite the same response. The bottom line is that little ones are a blessing to be around.

Now I would like for you to think about something for a moment. Brett and Christi are the main reason Charis exists today yet they get very little credit or acknowledgement. They care for Charis and nurture her as she is growing up. Now fast forward to the future. Let's say Charis is now a teenager or young adult. If a situation occurred and I needed advice, do you think I would look to Charis, or to Brett and Christi for the answers? Of course the advice and insight of the adult would be more meaningful and relevant. Because they have experienced more in life the wisdom and knowledge they could offer would be more beneficial. As great as goals and quotas are we can find out a lot more information from vision and insight.

Goals and sales quotas are very similar to vision and insight. However, there is one main thing that sets them apart. A sales quota is a set path to one destination and goal. You either get there or you come up short. There is no deviation from the plan set forth. Vision and insight allow you to see a bigger picture as many paths lead to a greater goal. I will try illustrating this concept to help make things a little clearer for you. When I first discovered vision and insight it was very hard to wrap my mind around them.

When you are in a sales presentation the goal is to make a sale. When you make the sale then you have achieved your goal. When I approach a sales presentation with vision and insight it is a bit different. I am focused on impacting the customer's life in a meaningful way, making a sale, building a customer base and finding a greater purpose and meaning. There is a big difference between the two. Vision and insight allow you to achieve many goals all in one experience. All you have to do is open your mind and see the bigger picture. I hope that vision and insight are beginning to become a little clearer as you read.

I want to take a moment and share with you what one of my sales presentations is like using vision and insight. When I greet a customer my first goal is to create a positive environment using passion and energy. Next I focus on relaxing them and building a bond of trust. Then I give them a show that is catered to meet their needs. Once their needs are met I begin building for the future. During the whole sales presentation I am looking ahead to see where the customer could take me with vision and insight. I am prepared to go left, right, or straight ahead in every aspect of my sales presentation. That is selling with vision and insight. Being prepared to take a course of action following whatever action the customer makes.

If you notice there is one main ingredient to all of this. Everything is designed to be about the customer. It all is based on allowing them to lead you as you guide them through their journey of the sale. This means that you are actually working for the customer and not yourself. The customer can fire you at any moment if they want to. This is something we often forget. How many times do you see a sales associate forcing a customer down a path they do not desire? That customer is going to fire you and you will not be making a sale. Even if you somehow make a sale the long-term vision of future business is totally gone.

I am sure many of you are starting to catch on to the concept of selling with vision and insight. Some of you may be thinking that this seems like a lot of work and is complicated. I am here to tell you that making the sale all about the customer can shorten your sale presentation and help you be more efficient. Everything I shared about my sales presentation can be achieved in minutes. I can create a positive environment, relax the customer, meet their needs and build for the future very quickly using vision and insight. It does not have to be a long and lengthy process.

So, the next time you enter a sales presentation I encourage you to enter using vision and insight. Make sure you are focusing and achieving many goals all at one time. Start seeing the bigger picture and prepare your mind for success. Be prepared to venture down any path that the customer may lead you that holds to the ethics and standards set forth by your company. When you do these things then amazing things will begin to happen in your sales career. You will find an abundance of blessings come forth like honor, respect, success, personal satisfaction and deeper understanding of the mysteries of life.

Chapter 13

Implementing What You Have Learned

During the journey of this book we have taken many paths and avenues in order to help us uncover the secrets to modern-day selling. My hope and prayer is that you take this new insight and create your own vision for your career. Make sure that you nurture and care for the seeds that have been planted within you so they will grow and be fruitful in the world of sales today. Use the self-examination skills to maintain your new-found success and seek the advice and knowledge of truth to have a firm foundation for the roots to settle in deep. This way when the storms of life pass by your skills will remain and continue to grow.

It is important to remember that your success is mostly based on you. What you put into your sales career is what you will receive. Make sure that you are productive and manage yourself well along the way. Be a presence that impacts your environment in a powerful way where people leave knowing they were in the presence of greatness. Take these skills and become a leader today that will transform this generation of sales associates and pave a path of truth for future generations. It all starts with an intense focus and desire for success which produces the passion and energy necessary to start your new journey to greatness.

There is one thing I stress that you must be mindful of as you move forward from this point. The insight you just received is exciting and contagious but there will be a time of testing. Because it is based on the principles of truth you will find yourself in a battle to hold tight to the core principles and values. As you move forward, things like fear and doubt will try to stop your growth. If you are not careful they will set in like a weed and begin to choke out the good that is growing in your sales career. Make sure you see these things clearly as they happen so you can prune your garden of truth as it grows.

Earlier I spoke about the sales associate who attends an amazing seminar and leaves full of passion and energy. They go back to their environment looking to be a difference-maker and success appears to be happening. Fast forward a few weeks or months and they are back to their old habits and bad ways. Nothing has really changed. They did not maintain their level of passion and energy because they allowed holes to appear in their mental passion and energy tank. It all quickly leaked away and they are left empty and desperate again.

Do not be this sales associate! Learn from the past and see these things before they happen. Seek out any holes that may exist in your mental energy tank and repair them with the self-examination skills you have learned. Take the time to fill up your tank on a regular basis with new knowledge, skills and insight. Remember that as you impact others' lives that you are gifting them with a free fill-up. Make sure you stay connected to the pump of truth so everything that flows from you is a blessing to others. When you base your sales career on truth you become a hot commodity that is desired by many. Stay humble, and continue to grow in truth, passion, vision and insight.

The key to successful selling is making sure that your motives are pure and proper. That you are there to serve your customer's needs no matter how small they might be. When you are able to do the little things with passion then big things happen. Throughout my career there are many success stories based on this concept. When you impact people's lives in a meaningful way, not expecting anything in return, success will find you. I will share a couple of stories from my selling career that are a testimony to this.

It was December 2009 and we were in the middle of the Christmas selling season. A young man entered the store and asked for pear-shaped aquamarine dangle earrings with lever backs. Christmas was only a week away. The store was packed and I had a decision to make. Take the time to custom-make these earrings for a small sell or simply pass and move on. I could tell he was desperate and time was running out. He had a specific need that was very important to him. So I took the time and ordered the parts and had his earrings waiting for him just in time for Christmas. He was happy and I felt good inside for meeting his needs. If he never returned again I can honestly say that it was worth it. However, this is just the beginning of every sales associate's dream customer.

Shortly after Christmas he showed up and purchased a Hearts on Fire diamond solitaire pendant and earrings. The sale was around $13,000 and was one of the easiest sales I had ever made. What I did not know was that this young man had invented a spinal piece used in surgery around the world. He owned his own business and was extremely successful. This was the perfect story of meeting your customer's needs and reaping an unexpected reward. However, the story has only just begun.

A couple of months passed and he returned to visit me again. This time he needed an engagement ring. Within thirty minutes he had decided on a $35,000 2ct radiant Tacori designer engagement ring. He paid in full without ever seeing the diamond. He trusted that I had his best interests in mind and knew that I was going to take care of everything for him based on the first experience we had with a $400 aquamarine earring set one week before Christmas. In just under a two-year span I have sold him approximately $140,000 in fine jewelry for his wife. When you do the little things right then big things can happen.

I understand that these things do not happen very often. However, just think of how much I would have missed out on if I had dismissed him on the first occasion. You only need a handful of customers like this to transform your sales career.

This is not even including all the little success stories you will create along the way. Even if I never saw him again I was satisfied within that I had impacted his life and made it better. That was good enough for me.

The next story I will share is one of my favorites. It was May 2010 and Mother's Day was right around the corner. A little boy arrived with his father looking to buy a Pandora bead for his mother. This little boy had saved what little money he had and wanted to pick out the perfect bead for his mother. So I decided to give him the ultimate experience. I put on a show that day for this boy and his father. That little boy left feeling so proud of his accomplishment and I was very pleased to have impacted his life.

What I did not know was the impact I had made on the father. He returned a couple of days later and purchased an emerald ring and earrings for his wife. He shared with me the impact that I had made on himself and his son. He could not believe that someone would take so much time and thought on such a small sale. I thanked him for sharing this with me. I told him how fulfilling it was for me to see his son smiling and full of confidence.

A few weeks passed and the mother came in to visit. She introduced herself and reminded me of the story of her son picking out her bead. She went on to share just how much my thoughtfulness and kindness had impacted their entire family. Since then they have shopped with us numerous times. The father returned for their anniversary and purchased a very nice diamond band. The mother and her older daughters come in together to spend quality time looking at Pandora jewelry together. It is always a pleasure to see them and it reminds me of the blessing that came forth from one small act of kindness.

These are great moments in my sales career that I look back on with fond memories. It is important to share that not all my fond memories have big sales attached to them. There are many acts of kindness that I have given that did not come with the reward of a sale but I feel just as rich inside. There is an elderly gentleman who comes to see me every time the time changes. He is unable to set his Rolex by himself and just needs a little help. He has no need for any jewelry and there never will be a dollar profit to be made from his visit. It is the inward profit that I enjoy, knowing that I have impacted his life and that he appreciates my kindness. These are the things that can fuel your passion and energy tank if you allow them to. It will sustain you and keep you going.

I think you now understand that the bottom line is that we are here to serve our customers and impact their lives in a meaningful way. If you approach your customer with this mindset, then success will find you in many different ways. In order to make these kinds of impacts on people's lives the process must start within your heart. When your heart is in the right place it will flow over to your mind and change the way you think and feel about sales. When your heart and mind are set together on the path of impacting people's lives then wonderful things will begin to happen. This is how you implement all the new skills and insights you have learned throughout this book.

I hope you have enjoyed this journey together into unlocking the keys to Modern-Day Selling. My prayer is that this knowledge and insight will impact your sales career in a powerful way. May it bring purpose and meaning to your life as a sales professional as you become a leader on the sales floor. You have a calling to be a light to others and bring purpose and meaning to their lives. I challenge you to become a part of this great revolution on the sales floor. Impact your environment and teach others the foundation of greatness.

For those of you looking for greater insight and success I encourage you to attend my Modern-Day Selling seminar. This two-day course is designed to share in depth each topic that you have discovered today. It is the road map for the modern-day sales associate to find lasting success and fulfillment. If any of you have a question feel free to email me at brian@moderndayselling.com. I will be happy to try to meet your needs. May you find great rewards and blessings through this message.

**BUSINESS
BOOKS**

Business Books encapsulates the freshest thinkers and the most successful practitioners in the areas of marketing, management, economics, finance and accounting, sustainable and ethical business, heart business, people management, leadership, motivation, biographies, business recovery and development and personal/executive development.